Relevance of the Liberal Arts in Twenty-First Century Academics

Notes for "Questionable Foundations and Quality in the Humanities," a Lecture by Dr. Marija Liudvika Drazdauskiene, Professor, Wszechnica Polska University, Warsaw, Poland Presented June 2014 in Lithuania

by
Thomas Langtry, B.A., M.A.Ed.
Director, Education Associates, LP
6750 Folsom Blvd., #230 | Sacramento, CA 95819, U.S.A.
www.edassoc.net | t.langtry@edassoc.net
Original date of completion: February 13, 2014

"Questionable Foundations and Quality in the Humanities"
by Marija Liudvika Drazdauskiene
©2017, *The American Journal of Semiotics,* DOI: 10.5840/ajs201721520
Reprinted with permission.

Table of Contents

Relevance of the Liberal Arts in Twenty-First Century Academics

This essay seeks to answer three related questions: Why has the liberal arts tradition fallen out of favor in the education profession? What does the evidence indicate regarding the results of this development? What evidence supports the argument that restoring the liberal arts foundation to education would benefit interested parties?

1. Why has the liberal arts tradition fallen out of favor in the education profession?

First, why has the liberal arts tradition fallen out of favor in the education profession? Reflection and research indicate some leading causes are the Industrial Revolution, widespread corruption, unregulated use of technology, and the development of a culture of superficiality as an alternative to intellectual development. Early education had basic, essentially unchanging components: the liberal arts; mathematics and science; the fine arts; and practical knowledge such as military, farming, industry, and domestic skills. These basic human needs and activities will never change; these complex interactions define human civilization. Although the basic components of human education cannot ever truly be altered, the volume of human knowledge grows more complex, voluminous, and difficult to master. So, too, the development of human activities has also grown more complex, from the discovery of fire and the invention of the wheel, to advances in farming equipment and techniques, to the development of industry and the introduction of technology. The various areas of human activity, like the various areas of human knowledge, are also more difficult to master, and equally more difficult to teach (Langtry, *Assessment-based instruction,* 2013).

Nonetheless, although human knowledge and human activity have understandably grown denser and more complex over time, the means of instructing students has scarcely changed. The very same pedagogical, lecture-based and dialog-based instruction methods that served since ancient Greece have proven every bit as effective in the modern world. Suddenly, however, the education profession has been calling for a sea change in instructional philosophy, insisting we introduce new methods of instruction so the new generation will develop the skills deemed necessary to survive in modernity. Malcolm Knowles' theory of andragogy, wherein the knowledge already possessed by students is considered more important than that possessed by the instructor, seems to call into question why we need instruction of anything (Langtry, *Assessment-based instruction,* 2013).

How has this change come about? The Industrial Revolution introduced mass transportation and mass production, and the resultant emergence of specialization splintered human knowledge, transforming education into an assessment-based, industrially driven, results-oriented effort. Contemporary learning is often not valued unless it serves a practical, industrially defined purpose, hence the emergence of assessment-based education. Coupled with the rise of consumerism these developments have spurred the evolution of an industry that unfortunately has devolved into a profit-driven game of statistical manipulation with the aim of enriching policy makers and education administrators and entertaining rather than teaching students. With the intended beneficiaries of education on the short end of this development, we have seen a decline in student performance during and after education. A sagging economy and rising unemployment, crime, illiteracy, and poverty rates serve as evidence. (Langtry, *Assessment-based instruction,* 2013).

Corruption plays a major role in our current dilemma. Assessments themselves do not thwart the purpose of education; they are an integral part of the education process as they allow for the measurement of learning. But assessment-based education is problematic. Currently, there is a "cart-before-the-horse" paradigm at play in which educators have to adjust instruction to ensure high test scores, with assessments apparently serving only to generate profit for the assessment industry. For instance, according to Suskie (2009), administrators should manipulate test results to elicit positive responses from selected audiences. Here are a few examples:

- "What If Your Audiences Will Feel Threatened by the Results?
  No one likes to hear bad news. People who are directly affected by assessment results—or might be perceived as having had a role in them—will naturally feel threatened if the results are disappointing… (Suskie, 2009, p. 278).

- "Offer Informed Commentary.
  Make clear the implications of your results…. Explain how the results answer the questions that formed the purpose of the assessment and how the results relate to college or program priorities..." (Suskie, 2009, p. 282).

- Create Specialized Reports
  "Sometimes one brief report won't meet all your audiences' needs. You may need to prepare a series of brief reports or presentations, each targeted to a particular audience" (Suskie, 2009, p. 284).

These are only three examples in one chapter of an approved academic degree program text. This chapter is dedicated to techniques intended to help the assessment community find ways to engineer assessment results for the purpose of financial gain. These methods do not serve the needs of students or the community in need of educated minds and people with the skills necessary to ensure the continued operation of a functional civilization. Restoring integrity to the education profession and maintaining standards and ethics and a dedication to the educational mission will result in assessments that demonstrate success, thereby eliminating the need to manipulate the results after the fact (Langtry, *Assessment-based instruction,* 2013).

The overestimation of the importance of assessment scores as a measure of educational attainment illustrates how political and economic interests have turned education into a game of pleasing students who want to be entertained; business interests who want to maintain property values; the political interests of appointees, and representatives; and assessment industry professionals. While these interests themselves are not necessarily bad or undesirable, expecting teachers, professors, academics, scientists, and scholars to dispense with intellectual rigor in favor of playing a servile role to students, administrators, and lobbyists does a disservice to everyone. Neither is this bleak picture an isolated view. The 2011 film *Detachment* portrays dedicated teachers in an American high school trapped between the corrupted motives of administrators and the distraught students experiencing the emotions of abandonment, betrayal, and anger at a fate they would not choose for themselves. In a scene depicting a meeting of teachers and administrators, views about misaligned priorities is given credibility:

"Administrator:

"Now, the one thing I've learned in all my years in the private sector is that real estate generates revenue and high property values will be this school's saving grace. But your school's low test scores are bringing down the whole re-sale value in this neighborhood during a market already in decline. We gotta get the scores up—new families in our district and more motivated kids in the school. And I am not placing any blame...

"Teacher:

"Excuse me, are you here to sell some test materials or to air your concerns as a property owner? This faculty has spent their lives on the boards, and now you tell us that our careers are about re-sale value" (Lund, 2011).

While blight and lowered property values are valid concerns, placing the burden for solving those problems on teachers is unrealistic, unworkable, impractical, and will ultimately only make the problem worse.

This concept of "teaching to the test" became infamous with the passage of the American No Child Left Behind (NCLB) Act. As with much legislation, this law was passed with good intentions. The performance assessments referred to in *Detachment*, to be fair, are designed to "motivate ambitious intellectual work" (Darling-Hammond, p. 642). Unfortunately, simply passing a law is insufficient; systemic problems involving endemic corruption and incompetence require a major commitment of time, money, and effort. In an analysis of NCLB's effectiveness, Darling-Hammond notes that American "schools are structured like warehouses, often housing three thousand or more students in an organization focused more on controlling behavior than on developing community. With schedules that cycle them through the classes of seven or more overloaded teachers and counselors struggling to serve the 'personal' needs of several hundred students, teenagers struggling to find connections have little with which or with whom to connect. Attending schools that are heavily stratified within and substantially dehumanized throughout, most students find themselves in uncaring or even adversarial environments. For adults, being accountable for the learning of 150 to 200 students daily is substantially constrained by the factory-model structure that gives them little control over or connection to most of what happens to their students" (Darling-Hammond, p. 643).

Nonetheless, NCLB offers a good foundation that appears on paper to be a workable solution for many of the problems described above. For instance, this legislation requires the presence of four basic components in the curricula of any secondary learning institute:

1. "Well-qualified teachers supported by ongoing peer collaboration and professional development.
2. Personalization achieved through teams of teachers working with shared groups of students ...
3. A common core curriculum organized around performance-based assessment, which engages students with work that resembles what they will do outside of school and challenges them intellectually (Lee, Smith, & Croninger, 1995; Newmann, Marks, & Gamoran, 1996).

4.   Support for struggling students to help them meet the demands of an intellectually engaging and challenging curriculum" (Darling-Hammond, p. 644-645).

The difficulty with this proposed solution is that all these elements amount to a basic description of what schools should already be providing by virtue of the nature of education itself and the existing laws that mandate educational institutes. That we need to pass laws to force schools to provide education is telling.

Darling-Hammond's criticism of NCLB goes on to cite problems with the current trend toward learner-centered, so-called "constructivist" teaching methods:

"[I]n a study of more than two thousand students in twenty-three restructured schools, Newmann, Marks, and Gamoran (1996) found higher levels of achievement on complex performance tasks for students who experienced what these researchers termed 'authentic pedagogy'—instruction focused on active learning in real-world contexts calling for higher-order thinking, consideration of alternatives, extended writing, and an audience for student work" (Darling-Hammond, p. 646).

Furthermore, short-sightedness on the part of lawmakers results in the corrupted use of laws like NCLB, as depicted in *Detachment*: "At the same time, the complicated rules mandated by NCLB have unintentionally made it more difficult for many heroic schools in low-income neighborhoods to do their work well and to keep the neediest students in school and moving toward productive futures" (Darling-Hammond, p. 646-647). Thus, NCLB exemplifies the problem with many approaches to solving our current dilemma: proposed solutions are good at diagnosing the problem and outlining a best-case scenario that would serve all interested parties in a perfect world, but too often the problems and proposed solutions are restatements of what we already know.

Looking at our crisis from a different perspective, mismanagement of public institutions is not a new phenomenon. D.H. Lawrence (1920) wrote about industrial management from the perspective of a family-owned mining company transferring leadership from an older to a younger generation. The heir to the mine made an early decision that he did not want to inherit along with the mine "an established order and a living idea" based on a "sacred foundation" of charity and "a unifying idea of mankind," traditional ideas that had guided management up to that point. Instead, the young heir, "somewhat shallow and uncaring," saw human concerns as nothing "more than a mental amusement," preferring instead to indulge in the celebration of "destructiveness for its own sake." The young heir viewed his employees not as noble workers, as had the previous management, but rather as "thousands of blackened, slightly distorted human beings with red mouths all moving subjugate to his will." Humanitarian interests, the entire subject of the previous generation of management, were to the new establishment wholly unimportant. In fact, "the whole democratic-equality problem [was dismissed] as a problem of silliness. What [mattered was] the great social-productive machine" (Lawrence, 1920). These prophetic words foresaw today's toxic environments in which even in the medical profession employees and patients are considered human capital, and that progress results from viewing human organizations in a cold and scientific light, with statistics and numbers as the only indicators of success (Langtry, *Psychomotor domain performance gap analysis,* 2013).

The explosive growth of technology further complicates the state of the education profession. The proverbial shiny object that never fails to captivate the attention of the otherwise disinterested subject has unfortunately become more of an obstacle to teaching than the useful tool industry marketing professionals intend. Even worse, the current trend to disregard everything not associated with the technology industry has severely weakened the fabric of civilization. In an article citing 33 reasons why the Internet will not render libraries and librarians obsolete, Sherman (2007) offers some insights about why over-dependence on technology harms the integrity of the educational environment. For example, the argument that the Internet's gift of universal information access eliminates the need to struggle through an arduous degree program is fallacious since "the notion that libraries are a thing of the past and that humankind has sprouted wings and flown into a new era of self-guided truth is nothing short of farcical" (Sherman, 2007, p. 24). Furthermore, the credibility of information on the Internet cannot be taken for granted. "The highly social nature of the Web...makes it highly susceptible to, for example, sensationalized, low-quality information with the sole merit of being popular" (Sherman, 2007, p. 24). Without the guidance of trained professionals who can ensure that students seeking a quality education receive fully vetted information and qualified feedback, the business community is left with a dearth of qualified professionals. In addition, "the Internet is subject to manipulation," and the search for information can be unduly "influenced by corporate interests" (Sherman, 2007, p. 25). While the "Internet is [not expressly] anti-intellectual [since] its academic roots (National Academy Press, 1999), and the immense quantity of scholarly sites...attest to it being a smart medium... [its] alluring immediacy...can lead to the false impression that only...interactive...and on-the-spot online discussion is of value" (Sherman, 2007, p. 26). And of course, "not everything is on the Internet" (Sherman, 2007, p. 26).

This trend toward oversimplification and superficiality has left us with glaring, seemingly unsolvable problems. First, because technological proficiency is already second nature to so-called "millennials," teaching young people how to use technology is redundant at best. More important, "Generation N" often does not have the skills necessary to enter the professional world, since they are lacking in critical thinking, linguistic, research, and math skills, and have not mastered identifiable areas of content knowledge, resulting in the cascading of social, political, economic, demographic, and cultural crises in which we find ourselves currently mired. (Conrad, 2008).

Perhaps most upsetting are the suggestions for how to address our current crisis, which amount to dubious solutions at best and fatal exacerbations at worst. Rather than remedying the established lack of commitment to encourage or even value intellectual development, many experts suggest we encourage greater dependency on technology. This suggestion is not intended ultimately to encourage intellectual growth now or in the future, but rather to steer young minds toward an increased obsession with popular culture, Facebook and Twitter chats, and assorted forms of intellectually empty activity (Conrad, 2008). Even more frightening is the conscious use of technology to engineer ignorance domestically while enabling the exploitation for production of people in countries with lax or non-existent labor and industry regulation to feed consumerism as a basis of domestic economic stability (Bitter & Legacy, 2008). Although one could argue that gaining proficiency in using technology to tame a difficult audience can enable a good educator to be effective in the modern world, merely keeping students calm with promises that classes will not challenge them beyond their ability to play video games is dangerous and irresponsible. By encouraging and fostering ignorance, the need for highly skilled and intellectually equipped people to fill the traditional roles necessary for the continuance of human commerce, whether for purposes of business, industry, political stability, or social and cultural enrichment, will go unaddressed. The future, while appearing bright and shiny from a distance, may in fact become a portrait of pain and human suffering, from which there will be no viable means of escape. (Langtry, *Psychomotor domain performance gap analysis*, 2013).

Table 1.1 presents a visual representation of the changes in classroom instruction methods since the 1970s:

Decade	Prevalent adult learning theories	Course delivery	Instructional tools
1970	Traditional pedagogical learning theories	Pedagogy, lecture	Lecture; Early audio-video; Subject Matter Experts
1980	Traditional pedagogical theories were still dominant, but increasing technology and modernization allowed less formal classrooms to thrive.	Pedagogy, lecture	Lecture; Audio-video; Subject Matter Experts
1990	Learner-based, activity-centered learning began to emerge.	Pedagogy, lecture	Lecture; Audio-video; Early modern technology
2000	Knowles	Pedagogy, andragogy	Lecture; Increasingly learner-centered activity; Technology-based learning
2010	Knowles	Andragogy	Technology-heavy; learner-centered; self-directed

Table 1.1: Historical analysis: Changes in teaching methods (Langtry, 2013).

Finally, the persistent celebration of popular culture has led to the insistent perception that postsecondary general education and related advanced courses are useless. It is difficult to imagine that anyone could argue against requiring general education as part of a curriculum; basic knowledge of mathematics, science, the humanities, languages, government, law, business, and art is the accepted method of demonstrating the right to participate in professional and business activity. Progress in business and the professions follows from one's ability to demonstrate growth in a given area, hence the need for students to select a major course of study, a minor course of study, and electives. With the overbearing presence of video game terminology permeating virtually every aspect of contemporary life, it is equally easy to know and difficult to understand why video game fanatics who understand the progression of multi-level games and "virtual worlds" that open up to them in direct correlation to their ability to zap electronic light blips on television screens for points in the video game fan community of their choosing cannot also understand the structure of secondary and postsecondary curricula requirements. Fueled with energy drinks and encouragement from social media networks to keep conversations light, superficial, and focused on popular culture topics like celebrity gossip, the picture of entertainment-overdose and entitlement among today's postsecondary student body appears even sadder.

Still, there are those who would argue that there is an alternative to the traditional general education and higher learning curricula, often stemming from a misinterpretation of the teacher's role. Chris Fosen (2006), in "University courses, not department courses: Composition and general education," details the behind-the-scenes complications and difficulties faced by university administrators whose staff's teaching methods represent controversial practices at best. Fosen offers these opening observations in tones that sound oddly critical:

> "Over the past century, general education's model of liberal learning has become so entrenched in U.S. universities that it is widely seen as the core of the national undergraduate curriculum. In a series of distributed courses that may continue through all four years of college, students engage in focused inquiry, problem-solving, collaborative work, and instruction in specific content areas, all to develop lifelong learning habits that prepare them for future roles in a democratic society" (Fosen, 2006, p. 11-12).

It is difficult to anticipate a rational argument to support criticism of a general education program that is supposed to exist. Some of this confusion may stem from the currently widespread culturally conditioned opposition to anything described as "liberal." Of course, the "liberal arts" are so-called because they are derived from traditional learning and teaching methods:

> "In medieval universities, the Trivium combined with the Quadrivium comprised the seven liberal arts. This teaching method is based on a curriculum outlined by Plato. One of the key intentions behind applying the Trivium and the Quadrivium is to distinguish between reality and fiction. By training the mind how to think— instead of what to think—this method provides a teaching of the art and the science of the mind as well as the art of the science of matter" (The 7 liberal arts, n.d.).

The current trend to oversimplify complex ideas has resulted in a reduction of the terms "conservative" and "liberal," in their contemporary political contexts, to vastly distorted significance with scarcely any real meaning at all short of supplying professional politicians, lobbyists, and propagandists with a way to decide with whom to agree or disagree without the trouble of listening or forming opinions. This practiced miscommunication further obstructs the irony of what Fosen is arguing in his journal article. Fosen takes issue with the provost's insistence that his composition courses meet the following criteria:

1. "Ability to select worthwhile subjects to write about and generate interesting ideas about them;
2. Ability to state a clear thesis, build support for it, and reach an appropriate conclusion;
3. Use of description, narrative, comparison-contrast, cause-effect, and other patterns of development effectively;
4. Ability to tailor writing to various purposes and audiences; and
5. Ability to edit prose to make it more clear, fluent, and concise and to minimize errors in usage, spelling, and punctuation" (Fosen, 2006, p. 15).

These guidelines are reasonable and in keeping not only with the function of general education requirements, but also with the stated purpose of composition courses—to teach students the skill of expository writing. As Fosen continues his narrative, his insistence that "liberal arts" programs are outdated, presumably because the current trend to ostracize "liberal" views, whatever that may mean, betrays motives that are far more radical and representative of a brand of left-wing extremism completely alien to even the most left-leaning of traditional liberal thinkers. Fosen hypocritically criticizes the criteria cited above as being in conflict with "accepted composition practice. It assumes a strictly linear model of invention, arrangement, and delivery that presupposes that students write to demonstrate their learning, not to learn" (Fosen, 2006, p. 15-16). Of course, composition courses are designed to teach the skill of expository writing, so what could the author be alluding to?

Fosen argues that "generating interesting ideas about worthwhile subjects and reaching appropriate conclusions about them in writing, all presuppose a legitimation process at work whereby teachers, not students, certify the knowledge that is allowable in the classroom" (Fosen, 2006, p. 16). In other words, Fosen believes that college level writing courses should be designed so that writing instructors can direct students to read instructor-chosen texts and express instructor-approved conclusions of those readings in instructor-approved terms, or more accurately, that composition courses should teach students what to write, not how to write. Such practices are closer to indoctrination than university education, and in the case of Fosen are driven by individual instructors' personally held beliefs, a situation postsecondary education institutes are designed to eradicate, not implement. Fosen's views are even more convoluted when you consider his endorsement of the view that free-market capitalism, a view normally endorsed by contemporary stereotypical conservatives, should be the guiding hand of the administration's management of core studies: "an educational, free-market approach that places student needs above disciplinary concerns" (Fosen, 2006, p. 14) is at the heart of his belief that teaching expository writing skills should be secondary to allowing instructors to create and sell their individual ideological agendas to their students, as long as the students seem to like it that way. At this point we have arrived at a state wherein universities are expected to propagate manufactured ignorance, and this is a very dangerous place.

2. What does the evidence indicate regarding the results of this development?

Second, what does the evidence indicate regarding the results of this development? A more detailed examination of the state of education reveals associated problems in several areas: the prison industry; messages from popular culture; funding, politics, and demographics; technology; mismanagement; violence in schools; reckless journalism; and deregulation. There may be no better place to start this audit than by looking at our current obsession with incarceration. We are all familiar by now with the former Soviet Union's history of gulags. Undoubtedly, in a country as vast as the former Soviet Union with an equally large population it may be reasonable to expect a higher per capita incarceration rate than in smaller countries. Furthermore, when the administration of a country is less democratic and more authoritarian, the potential for abuse may also be greater. But while many celebrate the fall of the USSR as representative of an end to extensive, reflexive imprisonment and suppression of individual liberties, many of these practices still continue. The February 2014 issue of *Harper's* includes an article entitled, "To the Penal Colony." In it, Masha Gessen (2014) details her coverage of a family visit to the incarcerated members of Pussy Riot, who were "were arrested in March 2012 and sentenced to two years in prison for 'hooliganism motivated by religious hatred,' after staging a performance at Moscow's Cathedral of Christ the Savior" (Gessen, 2014 p. 15).

It is probably a mistake to judge the customs and laws of one nation by the standards of another, so I will dispense with the debate about the rightness or wrongness of the crime these inmates were charged with. As this discussion unfolds, we will see that in some respects, what the State wants in this case may be in the best interests of the inmates. The author describes some of the artifacts in the waiting room:

> "One of its walls was entirely taken up with bulletin boards. A small one labeled, 'The Social Mobility System,' featured charts and flyers geared to show that 'malicious repeat offenders' would come to no good in prison, while 'positively characterized convicts have hope for the future.' A large board labeled Information was entirely covered with sample applications and other documents: an application to be granted a visit with an inmate; an application to have a package delivered to an inmate; excerpts from laws relevant to the business of visiting inmates; and descriptions of attempted violations colony authorities had successfully intercepted" (Gessen, 2014, p. 16).

Among the items the inmates' family members had brought were books:

> "Marchenko was a Soviet dissident who spent years writing this exhaustive accounting of the lives of political inmates in Soviet camps; he died behind bars in 1986, following a hunger strike to demand the release of political prisoners. Nadya had asked for this book specifically; Petya had been unable to find a copy for sale, so we brought the one from my personal library. Two human rights activists who had been helping Petya had added another eight books by and about dissidents. A Russian translation of a book by the philosopher Slavoj Žižek rounded out the list of ten books—the maximum number allowed at one time. Nadya had been corresponding with Žižek, and she had said she liked the idea of carrying on a conversation with the man and his

books at the same time. Months later, only the Žižek volume had made it past the prison censors" (Gessen, 2014 p. 17).

Politics aside, and looking at the charges, one could argue that the State is providing a service to misguided, overenthusiastic, and idealistic youth. To outward appearances, the "penal colony" wants the best for its inmates, even allowing them to not only read the published works of known dissidents, but also to correspond with them. It is important to note here that intellectual curiosity, the expected hallmark of university students, seems robust in a prison in Zubova Polyana, Mordovia, where the demand for works of known intellectuals exceeds the supply, whereas typical American university professors cannot force feed even the most basic and valuable of Western Civilization's intellectual treasures to paying students who regard such pursuits as beneath them and a complete waste of time.

Not to oversimplify, Gessen goes on to discuss the town in which this prison is located:

"The Zubovo-Polyanski District, of which the town of Zubova Polyana was the administrative center, was in essence a company town formed around the prison authority. A penal colony was the economic and architectural center of each village, with small, impermanent-looking wooden residential houses clinging to the colonies' concrete buildings and tall churches. I found one ongoing construction project: an apartment building for prison authority staff across the street from the district prison authority itself. The tall fence around the construction site and watchtowers in its every corner suggested that the building was being put up by inmates" (Gessen, 2014 p. 18-19).

On the other hand, if prison is such a prominent part of the landscape in this part of the world that it is considered the normal socialization process, there must be some serious societal ills.

Looking at this problem from an American perspective, we can see the same tendency for excessive incarceration. Darling-Hammond (2006) has already pointed out how too many American high schools serve more of a warehousing function than any real education function. In a sense, American high schools have largely been transformed into low-security detention centers, replete with armed guards and metal detectors. The American prison system, in many regards, is a much bleaker scene than that depicted in Gessen's (2014) article about the Russian system. In "Class, Race & Hyper-incarceration in Revanchist America," Wacquant (2010) describes in great detail the landscape from which many students emerge, and back into which many graduates retreat: "The single greatest political transformation of the post-civil rights era in America is the joint rolling back of the stingy social state and rolling out of the gargantuan penal state that have remade the country's stratification, cities, and civic culture, and are recasting the very character of 'blackness' itself" (Wacquant, 2010, p. 74).

Of course, education has always been offered as a way forward in the world, a means to a better life. Wacquant supports this view with statistics:

- "13 percent [of inmates] have some postsecondary education (compared to a national rate above one-half);
- The lifetime chance of serving time for African American men with some college education decreased from 6 percent to 5 percent;
- The lifetime probability of serving time in prison for African American males who did not complete their secondary education is twelve times that for African

American males who went to college" (Wacquant, 2010, p. 79).

Nonetheless,

> "the punitive and panoptic logic that propels criminal justice seeps into and erodes the shielding capacities of the welfare sector...by inflecting the practices of child protective services in ways that turn them into adjuncts of the penal apparatus, [undercutting] the educational springboard, as depleted inner-city schools serving a clientele roiled by mass unemployment and penal disruption come to prioritize and manage issues of student discipline through a prism of crime control" (Wacquant, 2010, p. 84-85).

Next, a brief look at American popular culture offerings makes it clear that a shift has taken place. The 1970's were perhaps the heyday of America's stature as international hero. Movies like *Bad News Bears, Star Wars, Willy Wonka and the Chocolate Factory,* and *Grease* and energetic and positive messages of what has become known as "classic rock" portrayed a societal innocence and absence of overt and absolute corruption expressed today by dark films like *Despicable Me, Kick-Ass, You're Next, The Social Network,* and rap music celebrating lawlessness, violence, and crime. Tom Wolfe in his recent novel, *Back to Blood* (2012), lays bare the underbelly of contemporary Miami in a darkly comic indictment of what the American dream has descended into: young sex addicts whose libidinous mockery infuriate the old guard, whose intelligentsia and professionals, infected themselves with decay and rot, suffer the abuse of the disrespectful taunting of once-or-future inmates whose incarcerations train them to acquire a sociopathic consciousness that is tone deaf to morality and responds only to the granting or taking away of material rewards in return for correct conditioned responses orchestrated by a law enforcement community beset with its own complicated rules of incompetence, greed, and vanity. Those of us who have refused to wade into this deliberately created toxic landscape of cruelty and injustice are aghast and disgusted at the destruction and misery that seems inescapable and the incalculable loss it represents. Could this be the cause of the inability of educators to recapture the attention of even the most willing of students?

Rhetoric and artistic representations aside, the statistics and demographics of this apparently unending nightmare have been documented. California's State Superintendent of Public Instruction, Tom Torlakson, writes:

> "California has the eighth largest economy in the world, yet faces sobering challenges to its long-term competitiveness. Too many working-age adults are ill-prepared for the demands of the 21st century workplace. Educational attainment levels are not keeping pace with the knowledge and skills necessary for complex, high-wage jobs that fuel the California economy; many adults lack the basic skills needed to ensure self-sufficiency. Further, underemployment and unemployment have devastating effects on communities as well as on individuals and the economy." (Torlakson, 2012, p. 1)

Torlakson's memo addresses the need resulting from California's current predicament in terms of education policies. For instance, the contemporary job market demands college educated professionals, many of which require a two-year degree. Foreign-born job seekers are increasing rapidly in California, more so than in the rest of the United States. As a result, while English as a Second Language (ESL) instruction at the community college level deserves funding and staffing consideration, problems with corruption, profiling, wealth distribution, and hyper-incarceration frustrate efforts (Torlakson, 2012).

An Associate of Arts (AA) Degree in English is a two-year degree and can serve the purposes of many job seekers. While the California Community College system makes this goal accessible to anyone meeting the very reasonable requirements for entry into this lowest tier of public postsecondary education, an ESL student attending English classes in an ESL program, even at community colleges, will not earn credit. Native speakers will likely not choose the English program, due to the problems described thus far, and if they can afford college at all, will likely place community colleges at the bottom of their lists because attitudes of entitlement cast community colleges in an undeservedly poor light (Langtry, *Action research proposal,* 2013).

Technology's transcendent influence, cited earlier as one of the causes for the devaluation of a grounded, liberal arts education, lingers after the fact as a further exacerbation of the problems associated with this loss. Some Information Technology (IT) professionals have publicly mourned their legacy of having created a generation without skills. This regret may not entirely be the result of deliberate maliciousness, though there is likely a good deal of bad intention at play. Sadder still, the idea of a "generation without skills" is not new. Martin Luther King, Jr., in a presentation in Atlanta, GA in 1966 entitled "The Social Activist and Social Change," noted:

> "…in the meantime we've got many human beings going through an inferior pipeline. We've got to do all kinds of patchwork and remediation to fix up what the schools haven't done right in the first place. We've got a generation without skills, increasingly incapable of standing on its own feet economically, in our kind of a

technological order. And what do we do with them? We need to transmit to these victims of inferior education basic skills and saleable skills with which they, if still educable, can make their own living." (King, 1966, p. 64).

Further, in a report by BBC News about an attack on tourists by angry mobs in Mozambique, Africa in 2008, Kgalema Motlanthe, Secretary General of the ruling African National Congress indicated that locals, "whose education was disrupted by apartheid," pushed out of their jobs by "better qualified" immigrants, were motivated by "'envy from South African sisters and brothers, who did not have the opportunity to acquire this education or skills. We need to address the young generation without skills in order to enable them to make a living'" (BBC News, 2008).

The advent of Internet communication has made circumventing the law all too easy and has enabled epidemic levels of mismanagement and bullying. Students know technology enables the attainment of material well-being without the unnecessary "busy work" of educating themselves, with the attendant tragedy that those who do bother occasionally find themselves displaced. Unfortunately, when these bullying tactics are brought to light, an admission of guilt is not normally offered as a promise to reform, but rather as an indication that hostilities, so to speak, are only getting underway. This practice of managerial bullying has been documented elsewhere. Work is supposed to be about producing quality goods and services. Living in a community is supposed to be about enjoying the benefits that result from living in accordance with this understanding. Gossip, rumors, and dishonesty should not represent the normal state of affairs. However, we now can see a persistent antagonism virtually everywhere and sadly, these stories have become routine. In Australia, for example, the normal happy rhythm of life seems not to exist anymore. A recent news article reports that:

- "A study found that misuse of social media infiltrates the workplace with often negative effects on employees' privacy, forcing many to switch off or limit their use of social networking sites.
- 8 per cent of Australian respondents discovered secret discussions about them online were initiated by colleagues using social media.
- 10 per cent have had embarrassing photos or videos taken at a work event and uploaded onto social media sites. This is as high as 19 per cent in Spain and 14 per cent in the UK.
- A small number of Aussie adults (7 per cent) even found themselves subjected to unwanted romantic advances through online media, and in the US this number rose to one in ten of all adults surveyed" (McKinnon & Boyd, 2013).

The prevalence of this behavior is disturbing. Its endemic presence is further evidence that the absence of a grounding in the liberal arts and the factual, historical, moral, political, and legal knowledge it imparts is potentially deadly.

Moreover, as the so-called War on Poverty takes on Orwellian overtones, local residents of Northern California, a generally affluent region, have been victimized by a combination of managerial bullying, misuse of technology, and the type of displacement mentioned in the example of the exodus from South Africa, above. Previously gainfully employed, many people have been displaced by out-of-state arrivals who, while not necessarily more well-qualified, use nepotistic practices and the misappropriation of corporate and government funding and personnel to remove already established employees from their positions. This well-documented abuse is discussed daily on American news broadcasts, often with the explanation that cost-cutting measures have resulted in downsizing due to problems with the economy. The perpetrators, who are usually proponents of a neoconservative "free market capitalist" view that "pulling yourself up by your bootstraps" is the way to demonstrate belief in the religion of capitalism, often are the recipients of the wasteful government and corporate spending rather than those they target as the dead weight necessary to provide prisons with the human capital required to feed the vicious circle.

There is also the undeniably disturbing trend of violence in schools. Historical records of school shootings in the United States date back as far as the 17th Century, at least. A quick survey of these incidents confirm what most casual observers would expect: over time, incidents of school violence have grown more frequent, more violent, and less comprehensible. The shooting in Newtown, CT, on December 14, 2012 claimed 28 lives, most of them children, and no comprehensible motive has yet been identified. With other notorious incidents like Columbine High School and the Virginia Tech Massacre in such close juxtaposition, no one can deny that something is wrong. (*List of school shootings in the United Sates*, 2014).

This problem has invaded all the parts of the world that we expect to function properly and depend upon most. Using journalism as an example, we can see that the post-modern constructivist mindset, in which one's perceptions and opinions serve as a substitute for fact, has led to recklessly inaccurate news coverage that has resulted in a misinformed population, again spreading the cascading and contagious toxicity of practiced delusion as an alternative to a rational world run by people in possession of a traditional education. In a review of Daya Kishan Thussu's *News as Entertainment: The Rise of Global*

Infotainment (Compton, 2009), Compton describes this phenomenon, "in which marginalized social actors are given voice and where vernacular forms of representation are afforded equal time alongside so-called elite discourse" (Compton, 2009, p. 178), as an indication that we have moved "beyond the debate about the 'dumbing down' of popular culture." Instead, we have created an industry of "'global infotainment,'" defined as "'the globalization of a US-style ratings-driven television journalism which privileges privatized soft news—about celebrities, crime, corruption and violence—and presents it as a form of spectacle, at the expense of news about political, civic and public affairs,'" (Compton, 2009, p. 178).

What got us here was a process of deregulation and privatization "aided by active state involvement...and the technological convergence of television, telecommunication and computing," (Compton, 2009, p. 179). Compton's book review makes the case that "the proliferation of crime, scandal and celebrity gossip has become 'a conduit for the corporate colonization of consciousness, while public journalism and the public sphere have been undermined,'" (Compton, 2009, p. 179). One chapter is entitled "War as Infotainment," and could be offered as proof that we have gone too far. This endless spectacle, pushed on affordable and attractive shiny electronic gadgets, designed never to sate, has stolen the attention of the world's population from a generation of genuinely caring and concerned educators and transfixed them instead on an unending flashing light show that steals from them their time, their identities, and their humanity and leaves the world cold, empty, and unresponsive (Compton, 2009).

Part of the promise of liberal arts education is that graduates will understand the importance of maintaining accountability and integrity at the highest levels of business and government in order to avoid the kind of catastrophe in which we currently find ourselves mired. Education is also a public trust, and deregulation has imposed itself here, as well. Practitioners of bad business practices, like the cave dwellers in Plato's analogy in which the true nature of reality is continually revealed to those living in conditions of ignorance and darkness, seem always to argue that the very practices that have been proven failures are really the right answers whose true benefit will eventually emerge. The accusations we have proven are the justifications they claim for their wrong actions. It is incomprehensible to the educated mind to use a known bad practice as a consciously chosen method, but such is the effect of ignorance.

Our *Zeitgeist* has been termed by some as The Age of Enron. The American Journal of Business has noted that:

"Before the collapse of Enron, many individuals and institutions in the United States, including representatives in the US Congress, were largely in favor of deregulation of business. However, in the wake of huge losses at the Enron Corporation, the debate on regulation vs. deregulation has been revived and gained momentum. It has become increasingly evident that corporate failure of the magnitude of Enron causes serious economic, political, and social dislocation" (Sridharan, U. V., Dickes, L., & Caines 2002).

3. What evidence supports the argument that restoring the liberal arts foundation to education would benefit interested parties?

Finally, what evidence supports the argument that restoring the liberal arts foundation to education would benefit interested parties? Misaligned cognitive theories, a decided lack of commitment, badly enforced regulations, and the whiplash brought on by the explosive growth of new technologies have resulted in a devaluation of what works. Thus far we have seen that while human activities and the foundations of civilized life and commerce have not, cannot, and will not change, we live in an age dominated by post-modern consciousness in which perception is sold as reality. Jürgen Habermas in *The Philosophical Discourse of Modernity* (1987), discusses this phenomenon as a persistent disruptive pattern of always unsuccessful attempts to construct a reality outside the established order that can be traced back to The Enlightenment.

While contemporary philosophers clearly have their say, this conception of the contemporary world also has its voice in education. B.F. Skinner is foremost among behaviorists, who experienced the height of their influence in 1950s and 1960s America. "Behaviorism is focused on the observable behavior of animals and humans. Effectively this means 'human actions are the result of prior conditioning and the way in which a person's external environment is arranged. Emotions, feelings, intellect, and so on are the means by which humans rationalize their responses to environmental stimuli' (Merriam & Brockett, 1997)." This era was followed by the influence of cognivist theorists like Piaget. Behaviorists argued that knowledge exists entirely outside the individual, who can be instructed with external motivators, rewards, and punishments, to learn to observe it correctly. Cognivist theory holds that the mind of the individual is the seat of knowledge, and that teaching and learning can only be achieved by attempting to help students learn to develop their intellect, which is informed by learning to understand the outside world according to established truths.

Malcolm Knowles' theory of andragogy has dominated the education arena since the 1980s. Pedagogy, a term loosely equivalent to lecture-based instruction, is etymologically related to the art of teaching children. Andragogy is a term coined by Knowles to address the very real differences between teaching adults and teaching children. Because adults already possess vast stores of knowledge, regardless of how it was obtained, Knowles rightly differentiated teaching adults from teaching children. His theory argues that what adults already know should be incorporated into the material offered by instructors in order to make the learning experience more relevant. As a result, Knowles argues, teaching adults should entail assisting learners in assembling, or constructing, new forms of knowledge from what they already know rather than the traditional form of pedagogical lecture, which strives to impart as yet unlearned factual knowledge (Knowles, 1980).

Constructivism, however, has proven itself a potentially dangerous theory. D.H. Jonassen (1999), in "Objectivism versus constructivism: Do we need a new philosophical paradigm?" asserts that "[c]onstructivism is a philosophy that views reality as internal to the individual, and that each individual constructs his or her own reality. It shares similarities with cognitivism; however, it differs from both behaviourism and cognitivism in the sense that it views reality as being not 'out there' but in the mind of the individual" (Hamat & Embi, 2005, p. 61). Clearly, when the education profession, and the community of philosophical, political, business, and religious leaders endorse a learning theory that pushes the idea of reality existing in the mind of the individual, the reasons for recklessly inaccurate journalism, a lack of respect for education in general, the profusion of popular culture artifacts like film, music, and fiction that celebrate psychotic and violent fantasies, and the endemic spread of corruption, ignorance, violence, and dysfunction become more clear. When a population of people, especially when the communication conduit is as powerful as the Internet, are informed that anything they think is reality, attempting to hold the attention of anyone in a traditional, lecture-based classroom in which participants are asked to accept an expert's views as superior to their own becomes difficult at best.

Thus, the advent of the constructivist learning environment has created a volatile and unstable situation in classrooms (and as a result in business and governments and communities) as places where teachers are expected to please students, rather than the other way around, and the expectation of parents and stakeholders are motivated by self-interest and the social realities of their "virtual worlds," which are in turn informed and driven by degraded popular culture created in a constructivist world view. There is an expectation that all students should always pass because there are no longer any right or wrong answers, only the responses of students whose perceptions, regardless of how misinformed, constitute a valid reality equal to any other by virtue of its constructivist "realness."

Fortunately, there are more than just the "big three" education theories of behaviorism, cognitivism, and constructivism. Oddly, we can see in the definition of the Trivium and the Quadrivium, that despite our contemporary worship of all things scientific, the ancient Greeks had formulated the rules and understanding of the human intellect long before Sigmund Freud and Carl Jung. These insights often shock those who mistakenly believe that the invention of the cell phone and the electric toothbrush indicate a higher degree of intellectual, social, and political evolution. However, the Industrial Revolution, as we have seen, has displaced and jarred every aspect of human civilization. To illustrate, the educational philosophy of Liberalism has been described as

> "the predominant approach in Western society. The philosophy dates back to the Greeks, where the approach was used to create a population which was intelligent, informed, cultured, and moral (Merriam & Brockett, 1997). The Liberal viewpoints, not to be confused with liberal political views, were the primary views in the United States education system until the mid-nineteenth century. Liberal arts education primarily revolves around reading books and discussing philosophy, religion, science, literature, the arts, and economics" (Zinn, 1998).

The earlier example of Enron provides a practical "real world" example of why re-establishing a traditional practice of education is necessary by illustrating the truth of the Aristotelian principle that a civilization that does not make the enforcement of its laws its first priority cannot sustain itself. Society exists to ensure the continuance of human commerce according to established laws. Sridharan, Dickes, and Caines (2002) provide the following description of how the American Securities and Exchange commission (SEC) is designed to serve that function:

> "The primary mission of the U.S. Securities and Exchange Commission (SEC) is to protect investors and maintain the integrity of securities markets. The SEC oversees corporate disclosure of information to the investing public. Public companies in the United States with more than $10 million in assets and whose securities are held by more than 500 owners are required to file annual and quarterly statements (Forms 10K and 10Q) with the SEC. These forms are supposed to disclose information about such public companies' financial

condition and business practices. This disclosure is expected to help investors make informed investment decisions. This SEC review process is intended to check if firms are meeting their disclosure requirements. The SEC seeks to improve the quality of the information disclosed and to help make a company's financial statements transparent, i.e., more easily understood by the investing public" (Sridharan, Dickes, and Caines, 2002).

Enron management sought alternatives to the normal, established vetting process in their investment activities:

"Enron's use of [so-called] "Special Purpose Entities" (SPEs) and the manner in which Enron accounted for them made Enron's financial statements very complex and difficult to understand. The SPEs also provided rich rewards to some of its officers, including the firm's former Chief Financial Officer (CFO), Andrew Fastow. Andersen performed both the external and the internal audits for Enron and also served Enron as a consultant in non-audit and tax matters. Andersen's three-way relationship with Enron created the possibility for several conflicts of interest.

"On the political front, Enron, its chairman Kenneth Lay, and its auditors contributed generously to the campaigns of many politicians in both major political parties in the United States (Watts 2001; Adamson 2002; Spain 2002). Its political donations may have given Enron some political power and some influence over the formulation of a U.S. energy policy favorable to the company. Despite its strong political connections and high visibility, the hazardous nature of its capital structure strategy and its risk management business essentially made Enron a firm built on very weak financial foundations....

"[Ultimately] Enron was forced to seek protection under Chapter 11 of the U.S. Bankruptcy Code on December 2, 2001. The firm was eventually de-listed from the prestigious New York Stock Exchange" (Sridharan, Dickes, and Caines, 2002).

The moral bankruptcy, selfishness, and short-sightedness that led to the demise of this corporation emerged in the environment that has stewed in the kind of irresponsible administration thus far outlined. While it is true that some people benefitted financially from this high-stakes confidence game, "[t]he sharp and sudden decline in the value of Enron stock adversely affected the retirement savings of thousands of ordinary Americans who had no direct connection with the firm" (Sridharan, Dickes, and Caines, 2002).

Comprehending the complexity and importance of the interrelationships among corporations, public trusts and institutions, ordinary citizens, and the balances of power in an increasingly global economy are the hallmark of the liberal arts degree. We all know from the global financial and housing crisis whose origins are usually placed in 2008 that none of us lives in a vacuum. The implications of Enron's failure are described thus:

"There are many levels of blame in this corporate crisis. Enron's top managers are clearly responsible for poor business decisions and mismanagement of the corporation. Not surprisingly, when required to testify before the U.S. Congress on the reasons for Enron's collapse, most of Enron's managers sought refuge under the Fifth Amendment. Decisions that individuals and corporations make often have multiple, systemic effects. Often, individual decision makers underestimate the consequences that follow from their decisions. When the governing bodies of corporations do not understand, or take account of all future consequences, serious moral hazards result. Messick and Bazerman (1996) argue that potential consequences are often ignored because of five possible biases: ignoring low probability events, limiting the search for stakeholders, ignoring the possibility that the public will find out, discounting the future, and undervaluing collective outcomes. It now appears that Enron management and the Board maintained all of the five biases to some extent. The many decision makers involved with Enron would have better served all stakeholders if they had considered the full spectrum of consequences associated with their decisions (Messick and Bazerman 1996, p.3)" (Sridharan, Dickes, and Caines, 2002).

Looking at the contagious nature of this kind of superficial understanding of how the world works from the viewpoint of academia, Iannone (1999) in the journal *Academic Questions* writes of professors who joke about doing "my Liza Minnelli routine," commenting on "the level of 'performance' expected of a teacher in the college classroom today" (Iannone, 1999, p. 14). She goes on to note the *Christian Science Monitor*'s descriptions of "colleges today" as "'expensive institutions competing primarily as youth resorts,' complete with 'pools, hockey rinks, catered meals, student centers, television rooms'" (Iannone, 1999, p. 14). Further, she notes the *Chronicle of Higher Education*'s comments "defending the old-fashioned lecture against the 'interactive pedagogy' in vogue today," as well as criticism of "student evaluations and their part in the 'dumbing down' of higher education" (Iannone, 1999, p. 14).

She also points to the destructive effects of reductionist teaching philosophy by referring to an article in *Harper's* entitled, "On the Uses of a Liberal Education: As Lite Entertainment for Bored College Students." Iannone (1999) reflects on the views offered by this article's author, Edmundson, about student perceptions of the liberal arts curriculum: already hamstrung by an administration who values the results of student surveys over the professorial assessments of student performance, she describes how "students fluently scribble their judgments of him, even those students who could barely fulfill the written requirements for the course" (Iannone, 1999, p. 15), resulting in Edmundson's admission that he is "'disturbed by the serene belief that my function--and, more important, Freud's, or Shakespeare's, or Blake's--is to divert, entertain, and interest'" (Iannone, 1999, p. 15).

Iannone's article goes on to offer the views of Kenneth R. Stunkel of Monmouth University, who "describes the new mode [of teaching] sardonically and well:

> "'Interactive pedagogy reduces the professorial role to 'facilitation' and 'partnership' in the 'learning process.' The professor becomes a congenial traffic officer...—as the cliché puts it, a 'guide on the side' rather than a 'sage on the stage'—while students supposedly learn from one another. In the interactive mode, students feel good about themselves because their views have as much status as those of the professor'" (Iannone, 1999, p. 16).

Further, "teachers who try seriously to challenge their charges may be courting trouble" because "there are ready ears all over the university to listen to their behind-the-teacher's-back complaints" (Iannone, 1999, p. 16). Referring to Edmundson again, she further cites the cause of this malaise as a collision of left-liberal politics and consumerism, with consumerism winning, Edmundson believes, "because demographic changes made the already expanded university a buyer's market" (Iannone, 1999, p.

17). The result is that university culture, "like American culture writ large, [has become] 'ever more devoted to consumption and entertainment, to the using and using up of goods and images'" (Iannone, 1999, p. 17).

This kind of passive aggression on the part of students not only shouldn't be encouraged in the first place, it cannot be allowed to continue. The example of Enron illustrates what happens when graduates unprepared to manage public trusts and institutions are placed in positions of considerable authority. Luring them to campuses with the illusion that the trouble-free and easy wealth that surrounds them during their four years of college, during which they are spoiled, pampered, pandered to, pleased, but never once challenged, is itself a crime of misrepresentation. The result is not only the imparting to students of unattainable expectations as realistic goals, but also the reality of creating Enron as a *de facto* business model that will continue to serve the very smallest percentage of the world's population while inflicting damage on the majority.

So, what is the alternative? Another teaching philosophy that is too often overlooked is objectivism. Merriam-Webster defines objectivism as: "1. any of various theories asserting the validity of objective phenomena over subjective experience; *especially*: realism; or 2. an ethical theory that moral good is objectively real or that moral precepts are objectively valid" (*Objectivism*, 2014). One could argue that objectivism stands in direct contrast to constructivism. In Iannone's words:

> "The breakdown of belief in an objective order of truth (again, truth not necessarily to be grasped but to be worked toward) and the loss of appreciation of the tradition that has however imperfectly attempted to embody it mean that professors have less of substance to impart; relativism ascends and the classroom becomes an open forum in which nothing real is at stake; students

become 'inclined to see the books they read as a string of entertainments to be placidly enjoyed or languidly cast down.' Since nothing is defended as being priceless, everything goes on sale and has its price" (Iannone, 1999, p. 18-19).

In this dark scenario that has already come to pass, the only beneficiaries of the consumer-driven policies that govern educational institutes are the corporate sponsors, lobbyists, policymakers, and assessment industry professionals themselves. The benefit to the students ends when they leave campus after four years. As for employment after graduation, presumably with firms like those responsible for these policies, the state of the education profession has been so crippled by irresponsible policies that genuinely concerned professors who attempt to challenge students to leave their "comfort zones" and master the content knowledge and communication and critical thinking skills necessary to be effective in the professional workplace only receive complaints from disinformed students who have already accepted futures as professional consumers. This is a dehumanizing and embarrassing footing for any civilization to consciously and deliberately propagate.

So, what do we do about it? In an article in *Library Review*, Joint (2007) argues that the current debate about whether the State's belief that it can make life better by passing laws often interferes with the very real possibility that laws actually can improve life. As we have seen with laws like No Child Left Behind, over-thinking a problem and trying to make laws that are overly-specific can lead to failure. Joint uses the examples of U.K and U.S. copyright laws. In the U.K., socioeconomic inequalities and technological development have resulted in copyright laws that take into consideration disability accommodations, the so-called "digital divide," intellectual property law, digital rights management, and reporting and record-keeping obligations. As a result, obtaining and getting permission to use copyrighted material from a library, with or without the use of technology, has become an overcomplicated obstacle course that defeats the purpose of granting Internet access to information in the first place. By contrast, the U.S. employs Fair Use laws, which apply a single agreed-upon set of usage rules to all forms of copyrighted material, regardless of who obtains them, how they are accessed, or for what purpose they are used (Joint, 2007).

Thus, this article points to two approaches to solving the same problem: how do we protect the financial interests of the creators of intellectual property without restricting its intended use? The U.K. attempts, albeit with good intentions, to address every conceivable possibility with volumes of legislation from every sector of human commerce, thereby inadvertently limiting access to information to which the legislation is designed to grant access. The U.S., on the other hand, understands the problem: to prevent unwarranted use of the intellectual property of others. As a result, universal rules determining how copyrighted material, regardless of media, can be used, were formulated, leaving the problem of access to those apparatuses already in place to address those needs (Joint, 2007).

Applying this reasoning to education, No Child Left Behind represents the same kind of "reinventing of the wheel" the U.K. displays in their attempts to manage the storing and distribution of information. Passing laws to instruct schools on the one hand to provide learning environments and curricula that should already be in place, then overriding them with complicated implementation policies that benefit corporations and corrupt political interests is self-defeating. We already have laws that dictate what constitutes an education and laws that dictate how educational institutes are to be administered. Rather than a new set of laws, we should enforce the laws that already exist. Administrations must commit to solving this problem. In the case of education, primary and secondary administrators must be empowered with the full authority to enforce laws that benefit students. In the case of universities, zero-tolerance policies need to be enacted. If students do not demonstrate the required competence to earn passing grades, they must not be issued passing grades. If student complaints are frivolous and have no basis in valid claims of staff misconduct, the complaints must be dismissed. Education policy, as the law already dictates, should be crafted without interference from private sector corporate interests, undue influence from the professional sports industry, or the corrupting influence of political lobbies. There is no need to change the structure of education. There is only a need to enforce the established order. We have seen that its alternative does not work; this discussion has provided ample evidence of how this precipitous decline began, where it has led, and where it will continue to lead.

Recalling Iannone's words that contemporary students are "inclined to see the books they read as a string of entertainments to be placidly enjoyed or languidly cast down" (Iannone, 1999, p.19), one might be tempted to describe our *Zeitgeist* not so much as the Age of Enron or the era of trading in what works for what sounds good, but rather as an unsettling time of seemingly incurable masochism. In this age, works like George Orwell's *1984* (1949) are regarded not as dire warnings, but rather as business and administrative models to emulate. A very generous assessment could describe this trend as the result of as yet misunderstood research from policymaking elite, but that would be a tough sell at best. In truth, this practice is a combination of incompetence, idiocy, and the opportunistic forces of corruption who are making the most of our refusal to act. The tools, the knowledge, and the skills to solve this problem have been in place since before the time of ancient Greece, but never before has a species practiced pseudo-ignorance to this degree of self-destruction.

Use the right tool for the right job. First, assessment-based education can improve the ability of educators to ensure that real, valuable learning takes place. Ultimately, a return to traditional education, with performance assessments viewed as the best indicator of educational success, is emerging. The need to understand that the results of the efforts of the education community are effective is not the problem. As a result, redesigning assessments and enforcing existing policies to ensure real student learning has become a priority. The development of competency-based learning (CBL) asserts that assessment tasks are most effective when they measure a student's ability to demonstrate competence in something perceived as worthwhile to the learner (Sluijsmans, Prins, & Martens, 2006). In addition, educators are reasserting so-called "alternative" assessments designed to demonstrate critical thinking skills by requiring students to produce knowledge rather than repeat facts as a preferred means of assessing student learning (Cummings, Maddox, & Richmond, 2008).

Second, technology is not in itself bad. Without technology, civilization would not be possible. However, misusing or abusing technology has demonstrably negative effects. Perhaps the most important debate of our time is that concerning the management of our natural resources. Two leading scholars in that debate each have published a book about the business of environmental resource management. Dambisa Moyo (2012) in *Winner Take All*, discusses the current trend of using technology to enable the proliferation of greedy and irresponsible exploitation of natural resources and the dire consequences in store for all of us if this abuse goes unchecked. Peter Senge (2008) in *The Necessary Revolution* details the efforts of corporations who are concerned about good corporate citizenship and the use of technology to ensure sustainability and the responsible management of public institutions and resources. Wall Street corruption is also made easier by technology experts who view integrity in business as an obstacle to profit, but as illustrated in the example of Enron, technology-assisted shortcuts result in greater losses than gains. Properly used, technology can aid in enforcing accountability efforts. Technology in the hands of contemporary students is a major distraction, and much of their refusal to make the effort to learn from what are perceived as obsolete books stems from their fear that they will not be able to put their love of using technology to use in their professional lives. Further, the proliferation of free applications and services has many young people mistakenly convinced that money is a thing of the past. Redirecting the attention of students to the fact that their passion for technology can be used to do real, important, and necessary work managing resources, maintaining infrastructure, and ensuring financial and administrative accountability can help dispel the delusion that professors who, to borrow more casual language, "are ruining their freedom by making them think too much, especially now that we have computers for that."

Finally, neither is capitalism itself a bad thing. Everyone likes the chance to prosper, attain wealth, and enjoy freedom and happiness. However, a corrupted application of this economic theory that forces a sort of slavery on the masses sold with an idealized misinterpretation of the free market has resulted in increased poverty, violence, and ignorance for more people than ever. Instead, the influence of the free market and the motivating power of consumerism can be used responsibly to enforce laws and policies that ensure professors regain control of their classrooms, administrations have the courage to enforce zero-tolerance policies, and students understand that getting an education takes effort that will pay off if taken seriously. For instance, charging for luxuries on campus rather than providing them for free can help train students to develop a strong work ethic and acclimate them to life after college. Further, administrations should reinforce high standards for entry into and graduation from college, including demonstrable evidence that applicants will take the work seriously. If students can't demonstrate competence in a particular class, students fail. If students file frivolous complaints, students should be disciplined. Standards should be high, and if students don't like it, staff and administration might remind them that while they may be paying tuition, a university is not a restaurant or a cruise ship, and the staff and administration are not required to entertain or please. No one forces students to attend. If a contemporary, tech-savvy student doesn't like academia, perhaps academia is not for him. Instead, such unhappy customers should be smart consumers and purchase tickets for a cruise or make dinner reservations at an expensive restaurant with the latest Facebook app.

References

Bitter, G. G., & Legacy, J. M. (2008). *Using Technology in the Classroom* (7th ed.). Boston, MA: Pearson Education.

Compton, J. R. (2009). News as entertainment: The rise of global infotainment. *Canadian Journal of Communication, 34*(1), 178-179. Retrieved from http://search.proquest.com/docview/219534837?accountid=35812

Conrad, D. (2008). Reflecting on strategies for a new learning culture: Can we do it? *Journal of Distance Education, 22*(3), 157-161. Retrieved from http://search.proquest.com/docview/214493124?accountid=35812

Darling-Hammond, L. (2006). No child left behind and high school reform. *Harvard Educational Review, 76*(4), 642-667,725. Retrieved from http://search.proquest.com/docview/212299060?accountid=35812

Drazdauskiene, M. L. (2017). Questionable Foundations and Quality in the Humanities. *The American Journal of Semiotics, 33*(1), 27-48. doi:10.5840/ajs201721520

Exodus after South Africa attacks. (2008). *BBC News*. Retrieved from http://news.bbc.co.uk/2/hi/africa/7414214.stm

Feiertag, J., & Zane, L. B. (2008). Training generation N: How educators should approach the next generation. *Education & Training, 50*(6), 457-464. doi: http://dx.doi.org/10.1108/00400910810901782

Finkelstein, J. (2006). *Learning in real time: Synchronous teaching and learning online*. San Francisco, CA: Jossey-Bass.

Fosen, C. (2006). "University courses, not department courses": Composition and general education. *Composition Studies, 34*(1), 11-33. Retrieved from http://search.proquest.com/docview/213784062?accountid=35812

Frank, T. (2011, August). Easy chair: The age of Enron. *Harper's*, Retrieved from http://harpers.org/archive/2011/08/the-age-of-enron/

Gessen, M. (2014). To the penal colony. Harper's, 328(1965), 15-19.

Habermas, J. (1987). The philosophical discourse of modernity. Cambridge, MA: MIT Press.

Hamat, A., & Embi, M. A. (2005). The application of learning theories to the design of course management systems. *International Journal of Pedagogies & Learning, 1*(2), 57-64.Retrieved from http://search.proquest.com/docview/893908062?accountid=35812

Iannone, C. (1999). Turning from truth to more dubious pursuits. *Academic Questions, 12*(2), 14-23. doi: http://dx.doi.org/10.1007/s12129-999-1054-y

Joint, N. (2007). Can new laws make public services better? Reflections on diversity legislation for libraries. *Library Review, 56*(5), 359-370. doi: http://dx.doi.org/10.1108/00242530710750554

Jonassen, D. H. (1991). Objectivism versus constructivism: Do we need a new philosophical paradigm? Educational Technology Research and Development, 39(3), 5-14.

King, Jr., M. L. (1966). *The social activist and social change...* Conference on social change and the role of behavioral scientists, Atlanta, GA. Retrieved from http://files.eric.ed.gov/fulltext/ED021926.pdf

Kirschner, P., Sweller, J., & Clark, R. (2006). Why minimal guidance during instruction does not work: An analysis of the failure of constructivist, discovery, problem-based, experiential, and inquiry-based teaching. *Educational Psychologist, 41*(2), 75-86. Retrieved from http://projects.ict.usc.edu/itgs/papers/Constructivism_Kirs chnerEtA1_EP_06.pdf

Knowles, M. (1980). *The modern practice of adult education: From pedagogy to andragogy.* Wilton, CT: Association Press.

Langtry, T. R. (2013). *Action research proposal.* (Unpublished master's thesis, University of Phoenix).

Langtry, T. R. (2013). *Assessment-based instruction.* Informally published manuscript, Education, University of Phoenix, Sacramento, CA.

Langtry, T. R. (2013). *Historical analysis table.* Informally published manuscript, Education, University of Phoenix, Sacramento, CA.

Langtry, T. R. (2013). *Psychomotor domain performance gap analysis.* Informally published manuscript, Education, University of Phoenix, Sacramento, CA.

List of school shootings in the United States. (2014). Retrieved from http://en.wikipedia.org/wiki/List_of_school_shootings_in _the_United_States

Lund, C. (Writer) (2011). Detachment [Theater]. Available from http://www.springfieldspringfield.co.uk/movie_script.php ?movie=detachment

Lynette, M. G. (2008). A study of teacher perceptions of instructional technology integration in the classroom. *Delta Pi Epsilon Journal, 50*(2), 63-76. Retrieved from http://search.proquest.com/docview/195592643?accountid =35812

McKinnon, M., & Boyd, S. (2013). *Social media stokes workplace privacy fears in Australia*. Retrieved from http://www.cio.com.au/mediareleases/15671/social-media-stokes-workplace-privacy-fears-in/

Merriam, S. B., & Brockett, R. G. (1997). The Profession and Practice of Adult Education. San Francisco: Jossey-Bass.

Moyo, D. (2012). *Winner take all: China's race for resources and what it means for the world*. Perseus, PA: Basic Books.

Objectivism. (2014). Retrieved from http://www.merriam-webster.com/dictionary/objectivism

Orwell, G. (1949). *1984*. London: Secker and Warburg.

The 7 liberal arts—trivium, quadrivium and logical fallacies. (n.d.). Retrieved from http://www.matrixwissen.de/index.php?option=com_content&view=article&id=275:the-7-liberal-arts-trivium-quadrivium-and-logical-fallacies&catid=145:die-7-freien-kuenste&Itemid=124&lang=en

Senge, P. (2008). The necessary revolution. New York, NY: Random House, LLC.

Sherman, W. (2007). Are librarians totally obsolete? 33 reasons why libraries and librarians are still extremely important. *Teacher Librarian, 35*(1), 21-27. Retrieved from http://search.proquest.com/docview/224886335?accountid=35812

Sridharan, U. V., Dickes, L., & Caines, W. R. (2002). The social impact of business failure: Enron. *American journal of business, 17*(2), Retrieved from http://www.bsu.edu/mcobwin/ajb/?p=199

Stiggins, R. J. (1991). Facing the challenges of a new era of assessment. *Applied Measurement in Education, 4*(4), 263-273.

Torlakson, T. California Department of Education, Executive Office (2012). Adult education planning document— linking adults to opportunity: Transformation of the California Department of Education Adult Education Program. (SBE-002). Retrieved from: https://www.cde.ca.gov/be/pn/im/documents/memo-ssssb-cssaed-apr12item01.doc

University of Phoenix. (2013). Historical Analysis Template. Retrieved from University of Phoenix, AET531 website.

Van Fleet, D., D., & Van Fleet, E., W. (2012). Towards a behavioral description of managerial bullying. *Employee Responsibilities and Rights Journal, 24*(3), 197-215. doi: http://dx.doi.org/10.1007/s10672-012-9190-x

Wacquant, L. (2010). Class, race & hyperincarceration in revanchist America. *Daedalus, 139*(3), 74-90,146. Retrieved from http://search.proquest.com/docview/744236690?accountid=35812

Wolfe, T. (2012). *Back to blood.* Little, Brown and Company.

Zinn, L. (1998). Identifying your Philosophical Orientation. Adult Learning Methods. Malabar: Krieger Publishing Company.

Zinn, L. (1998). *Philosophy of adult education.* Retrieved from http://www.labr.net/apps/paei/

Appendix: Lecture by Prof. Drazdauskiene

Questionable Foundations and Quality in the Humanities

Marija Liudvika Drazdauskiene, Wszechnica Polska, Warsaw

Reprinted with permission.

1. The problem and its context. With the set of subjects still bearing resemblance to the Renaissance humanities when this concept for a programme of learning (*studia humanitatis*) was created (Ulčinaitė, 2011), the humanities today have become a somewhat dishevelled programme, although the European humanities have much in common with the American liberal arts and they do suffer similar grievances.

The classical *septem artes liberalis,* which included grammar (language), dialectics and rhetoric as *trivium,* and arithmetic, geometry, music and astronomy as *quadrivium,* had been the studies "available to and pursued only by free men, materially and spiritually" (Zabulis, 1995; Ulčinaitė, 2011) and were inherited by the Middle Ages. Yet, in classical antiquity, liberal arts were the studies of free cultivated men who desired to achieve intellectual elevation and refinement, to speak well and convincingly, to be able to imitate the classical authors aided by the excellent knowledge of Latin, Greek and Hebrew. In the Middle Ages the *Trivium* and the *Quadrivium* taught how to think instead of what to think when the method provided "a teaching of the art and the science of the mind as well as the art of the science of matter" (The 7 liberal arts, n.d. In: Langtry, 2014, 14). However, at present, the time-tested belief that the humanities are the acme of education no longer seems to be true. Although tentative suggestions to the contrary have been heard recently[1], the same source deplored that "there is very little interest left in

---

[1] Cf.: "… if what is deemed as "socially relevant" or with social impact is qualified in terms of material things/results, then this is very far from the purpose of these disciplines" ("And your relevance is…?" – 'Humanities Today' by Alexandra Ion (Rumania) // www.academia.edu – Retrieved 1 March 2013).

reflective approaches on what it means to be human, on values, virtues and things related. And these are the fundamentals of what make us and our disciplines. It would be futile to answer the question "why is poetry needed or opera?"" (Ibidem).

The notion that the humanities have been compromised is obvious from the fact that even subjects of classical studies, such as the literature of classical antiquity, Latin and Greek, are squeezed into the minimum of hours in universities. The humanities as the programmes of modern languages and literatures have also diminished at the expense of subjects of practical skills introduced to buy off at least the minimal existence of language and literature studies. Administrators seem to be indifferent in stringent financial circumstances while young students follow in the wake of their pragmatic parents. I intend to question **what** has changed in the humanities and **whether** people in education have not contributed to the result as it is. Finally, **what cultural values** are embedded in and must be retained for the upkeep of the humanities today?

2. Highlights in reality that indicate the status of the humanities in the world.

A similar situation has been found in the United States, as described and argued about by Thomas Langtry in his analytical paper (Langtry, 2014). This researcher points out the following flaws: 1)disregard to the education of informed and intellectually ready person able to think critically, to select and evaluate what is created in the country and in the world (emphasis MLD) and what is offered as products of popular culture and to be accountable while tailoring courses and instruction in colleges and higher schools "to propagate manufactured ignorance" (Langtry, p.16), to subject the students too slavishly to prescribed reading and to "instructor-prescribed conclusions" (Langtry, p.16), which is "closer to indoctrination than university education" (p.16); 2) "over-dependence on technology" which "harms the integrity of the educational environment" (p.9); 3) "the current trend toward learner-centred, so-called "constructivist" teaching methods" (p.8); 4) the discarded or missing principles of humanistic education and of its aims, of a resort to historical results and value of the humanities. Specific

American issues highlighted in Thomas Langtry's paper include financial mismanagement in American schools, academically overstretched teachers, online abuse and otherwise flawed behaviour, violence in schools, penalty system in America (p. 17, 20-21), degraded morality which can questionably be "an issue of degraded principles in education" (p.21-22) and other matters.

The situation in the humanities is very much alike the world over. A recent publication on the Internet, 'The Wrong Way Corrigan', reports on the inflated standards in assessment in the humanities "in Colombia's highest-rated university – Los Andes" where lecturers are compelled not to fail those students who deserve to be failed because they are "too big to fail" and where the standard marking 'procedure' "is adjusted to see them 'right'". Cases have been reported in Los Andes when a female student, "who barely turned up all term", went ":berserk" in front of a professor when she realised she could fail and won a pass.

People in Colombia's Los Andes appear to differentiate between 'qualification' and 'education'. In accord with the definition, "qualification is a result, while education is a process". These concepts help Columbian professors navigate between professional commitments and lenience to the students while they alleviate conditions for the obtaining of a diploma.

People in the humanities in Lithuania will recognise that such matters as the treatment of instruction as irrelevant, lenient requirements to the students, criteria of evaluation, the flawed role of instructor/lecturer and that of the student in education, which Thomas Langtry finds typical of American education, are very much home-sounding in Lithuania.

Similar and newer vices beset students in East European universities. Plagiarism and purchased academic papers, which inflate education considerably, are widely spread in the humanities in this age of technology in Eastern Europe. Sometimes it is impossible to identify the authorship of a student's paper copied from Internet sources, but sometimes this is obvious. Yet academic heads and administrators refuse to lower the mark to the dishonest students or fail them because there is no material evidence of plagiarism but the experienced lecturer's evaluation, and because "plagiarism is a scourge of all universities, even of those in the West today". Thus, the lecturer's knowledge, experience and requirements are ignored, while the student gets a pass and a diploma on the basis of a paper in which his mind produced no line.

Present-day paradoxes have considerably distorted the idea of the humanities and created the situation as if their foundations have become questionable. For example, the right yet overemphasized promotion of intellectual readiness and judgmental ability over information in higher education, although put forward by the first persons in the Lithuanian Republic, such as Academicians Jonas Kubilius and Henrikas Zabulis in the 1980s, has been taken to extremes, was distorted and lost its significance. History and tradition inherent in literary studies have lost to novelty which has been turned into "an orgy of ignorance". Whether through pleasure or profit, methodological innovations and technology have become things desirable in themselves rather than factors to be internalized and integrated before they are acquired. Like Thomas Langtry, I discern a vice in emphasis on technology *per se*, which has been taken to absurd lengths so that it started reminding of William Cowper's evaluation in his poem of the 18th century: "(pleasure)*That ruling goddess..., still leaning on the arm / Of novelty, her fickle and frail support...*" (William Cowper. *The Task,* Bk.III, 53-54). Science has lost to fashion and dignified instruction to a show-style performance down to the disgrace of the teacher, with psychological comfort, pleasure and motivation shifting the gears in relations in education.

3. The retained structure of the humanities and the relevance of the semiotic approach. Leaving the final evaluation of the status of the humanities in Lithuania for the closing section in this paper, I should like to draw attention to the difference of the subjects in the humanities today and in the antiquity, in the number of students and of requirements to them. We have to notice the depth in learning, especially in the learning of languages, then and now, and the numbers.

I should like to analyse the present state of the humanities from the semiotic perspective while viewing education as an integrated aspect of communication.

Taking short cuts, I have borrowed my basic concept explaining the relevance of semiotics to the present paper from a seminal book published about a century ago:

"All experience is enjoyed or interpreted... or both. ...very little of it escapes interpretation. ... An account of the process of interpretation is thus the key to understanding of the sign-situation, and therefore the beginning of wisdom" (Ogden & Richards, 1923/1960, 50)[2]

The basis of the account of interpretation is, to Ogden and Richards, "the fact that experience has the character of recurrence, that is, comes to us in more or less uniform contexts", which are more or less distanced in time, and "this is all that is required for the theory of signs" (p.55). The problems that encumber the interpreter and his account are basically linguistic. Ogden and Richards were saying that natural human language is the basic and important medium in science, but, in communication, it is beset with superstitions and inaccuracies. The inaccuracy of natural human language has been a problem to scholars and scientists and the call for the scientifically infallible language has been known from Ogden and Richards, Bertrand Russell, Roland Barthes and Algirdas J. Greimas, Daniel Chandler and may other researchers.

Like many semioticians and some sociologists, I have chosen to treat education in the humanities (and other fields) as communication, which is recognized in semiotics and is in line with the models of communication defined it in. To explain the codes which develop in communication and textual interpretation (Chandler, 2007, 175-190), the initial reference is to the much quoted and widely known Jakobson's model of communication[3]

---

[2] My references to Charles Ogden and Ivor A. Richards here and further have been chosen for their comprehensive and essential relevance as for their condensed sense, which may have been reiterated in fragments in different new authors but which have also lost much of their infallible clarity in the later authors.

[3] This model includes: Addresser (the emotive f.), Addressee (the conative f.), Context (the referential f.), message

(the poetic f.), contact (the phatic f.), and code (the metalingual f.) (Jakobson, 1960/1966, 357). This is a simple enough and comprehensive scheme, although it may be modified when the functional theory of language (Halliday, 1973, 1976) is taken into account and when imaginative literature is in focus in research (cf. Widdowson, 1992; Drazdauskiene, 2011, 42-84, esp. 81).

(Jakobson, 1960; Lotman, 1992/2004, 39-41; Chandler, 2007, 180-186). Time nor space permitting an elaboration of this scheme in linguistics and semiotics, historically and synchronically, only its components in their terminological sense and the codes that this scheme indicates and that develop in communication are relevant to my presentation. "A code is a set of practices familiar to users of the medium operating within abroad cultural framework" whose conventions "represent a social dimension in semiotics" (Chandler, 2007, 148). The basic code and the one that causes most problems in semiotics, as I have mentioned above, is language, and language will be my basic concern in the present paper.

To place the question of language in context, my reference is to an inventory of codes in verbal communication recognized in semiotics: social codes (verbal language, bodily codes, commodity codes, behavioural codes), textual codes (scientific, aesthetic, genre, rhetorical and stylistic, mass media codes) and interpretive (perceptual and ideological codes) (Chandler, 2007, 149-150) for the initial evaluation of the material. It was yet Algirdas Greimas who indicated the relevance of these concepts in the interpretation of culture, communication and ideology (Greimas, 1971, esp. 41-48). In particular, Greimas considered that every system makes sense if it is realised in active processes. In culture, which is a system of values, it is relevant to differentiate a system of values in the abstract, or axiology, and a system of values as a model of behaviour, or ideology. Minding that Greimas called for "to describe culture with insights into its deep levels and to formulate logical axiological systems for cross-cultural comparisons" (Greimas, 1971, 48-49), I shall resort to culturally relevant generalizations in my analysis and conclusions.

4. The view of language and communication that has remained relevant for years. The codes enumerated above indicate the presence of language in the codes of all types. As the basic medium in the humanities featuring in all of the codes above, language is "the richest system of meanings" and values (Greimas, 1971, 41) and should be evaluated in my argument. As far back as the 1920s, Charles Ogden and Ivor A. Richards drew attention to the flawed use of natural human language, which obstructs both communication and scholarship, as they emphatically reiterated. Assuming that "symbols (i.e. words and propositions or sentences) cannot be studied apart from references which they symbolize" (Ogdden & Richards, p. 223) and that the expression of attitude is intrinsic in speech, they identified the symbolic and the emotive functions present in each instance of the use of words, and claimed that reference is present in "almost "all use of words" of "civilized adults" (Ogden & Richards, 150; cf.: Halliday, 1976, 20). They insisted that these functions (of words) should not only be kept apart in intelligent communication, but that communication should be tested for them. They advised to check whether the question, *"Is this true or false in the ordinary strict scientific sense?"* applies to the language used: if this question is relevant, we have the symbolic use of words, if it is irrelevant, the emotive use of words (Ogden & Richards, p.150). When we determine whether we deal with the symbolic or emotive use of language and give an account of interpretation in causal terms, we may notice "the beginning of a division **what cannot be intelligibly talked of and what can"** (Ogden & Richards, p.vii). This is the assessment which is so relevant to communication today and which <u>points directly to the quality of communication in the humanities</u>. These authors, then, warned **against the emotive use of words** and **against images**, i.e. "those revivals or copies of sensory experience which figure so prominently in most accounts of thinking" (Ogden & Richards, p.59-60) and which are irrelevant in the account t of communication and the theory of signs, one of which is language.

Another irrelevant factor is the superstition that "words are parts of things and always imply things corresponding to them", which does disservice to the symbolic uses of language especially evident in philosophy (Ogden & Richards, p.14). American authors have written extensively on this issue in the middle of the twentieth century[4]. Daniel Chandler, who complained that "So

---

[4] Charles K. Ogden and Ivor A. Richards were aware of this fallacy and defined relations between words and things. In the triangle of thought, words and reference, as defined by Ogden and Richards, there is no causal relation between symbol and referent, yet this relation should not be ignored in a discussion of meaning; the use of words is merely symbolic (or arbitrary, in contemporary terms) and this relation cannot be verified. The

much of what is written about semiotics is written as if to keep out those who are not already 'members of the club' (Chandler, p.xiii), has a lengthy section entitled "The word is not the thing", which means that the fallacies identified long ago persist in verbal communication. If the non-identity of words and things and their arbitrary relations are ignored or confused, confusion issues in communication, which is to be avoided in science and philosophy. This takes me directly to the object of study in my presentation.

5. Bertrand Russell's requirements to the language of science.

Questions of language and science were analysed and taken further in a different framework by Bertrand Russell (Russell, 1965). Initially, he made a few concrete observations. Like Ogden and Richards before him or Greimas and Barthes after him, Bertrand Russell pointed out the inaccuracy of natural human language[5] which can conceal our thoughts and state falsehoods. He made a distinction between language of lowest order or 'object language' and languages of higher orders. In the former, 'object words' are essential and the distinction "between sentences and single words does not exist": each word means "a sensible object"; this meaning does not depend upon their occurring in sentences", and "each word is an assertion" (p.17, 26). The words 'denotes' or 'means' apply to this kind of language (p.17, 26). "Words in languages of higher orders 'mean' in other and much more complicated ways". Words 'true' and 'false' belong to a language of higher order (p.17). It may be assumed that **awareness of 'object words' in their present**

---

relation between thought and referent (or thing) is more or less direct, (e.g. when we think 'Napoleon'). This relation can be measured in terms of adequacy (small wonder scientists may speak the same language with common men, but they assume=understand different things and processes under the same words) (cf.: (Reference)" ... as a set of external and psychological contexts linking a mental process to referent. ...it is unlikely that any two references will ever be strictly similar. ... It is better to ask whether two referents have sufficient similarity to allow profitable discussion." Ogden & Richards, pp. 90-91). The relation between thought and symbol is causal and can be measured in terms of correctness (correct/incorrect) (Ogden & Richards, p.11).

5 „One of the difficulties of the subject is that we have to use common words in precise technical senses which they do not commonly bear;..." (Russell, 1965, 16).

definition may literally guide in teaching while assessing students' knowledge at the initial stages of learning.

Another distinction made is between words and sentences: words mean and sentences signify[6] to Bertrand Russell (p. 158). In 'object language' "each word is an assertion" (p.17). Anything beyond assertion or relatedness of non-linguistic occurrences to statements "can only be effected by means of sentences" (p.26). "An indicative sentence 'expresses' a state of the speaker, and 'indicates' a fact or fails to do so" (p.203). Sentences in logic and mathematics can contain no object words. In all other spheres, including theory of knowledge, object words have a function. On pursuing the idea of the unambiguous language of science and on assessing, self-critically, that what is said in the initial chapters of his book "has not the degree of precision sought in later chapters" (p.17), Bertrand Russell showed that the absolutely neutral language of science is hard to achieve. Charles K. Ogden and Ivor A. Richards acknowledged this difficulty (Ogden & Richards, p.195) before him and Algirdas J. Greimas after him (Greimas, 1977, 78-80; 1985, 32).

6. Key questions of epistemology. Bertrand Russell's greatest merit is his account of the questions related to the intersection of language, experience and logic. Focusing on the principal questions of epistemology (or theory of knowledge), he analysed principles that govern the use of language as we attempt to record experience. He also attempted to give an answer to a key question, such as 'Why should I believe unquestionable truths, such as the truths of mathematics like $7 \times 8 = 56$?' This is the question of the first form of epistemology. It rises from our acceptance of the scientific account of the world "as the best at present available" (Russell, 1965, 14, 10). It questions what sort of phenomenon an account represents and how that account compares with our perceptive awareness and habit-knowledge,

---

[6] Cf.: "Whether or not there is a substantive 'significance', there is certainly an adjective 'significant'. I apply this adjective to any sentence that is not nonsense. 'Significant' and 'significance' are words that I apply to sentences, whereas 'meaning' is a word that I apply to single words. This distinction has no basis in usage, but it is convenient. When a sentence is not significant, I call it 'nonsensical' (Russell, 1965, 158).

which together constitute knowing (p.11)[7]. An individual's experience becomes relevant here as a source of knowledge, which is significantly determined by the influence of signs. To Bertrand Russell, "language is a species of the genus 'sign'", which takes part in recording man's experience (p.12). This causes linguistic problems and introduces additional concepts into the argument. The behaviour of an organism under the influence of signs raises the question of the distinction between 'subjective' and 'objective', between 'knowledge' and 'error', which Bertrand Russell described for the first form of epistemology (p.12).

However, when man considers how he perceives occurrences in the outside world, it becomes relevant to question whether the observer perceives and records the objects and occurrences or only the effects of the observed objects upon himself. Paradoxically, when science "most means to be objective, it finds itself plunged into subjectivity against its will", as the question remains whether the observer "is recording observations about the outer world, (or) is really recording observations about what is happening in him" (p.13). The question, then, is, "what passes as knowledge", and this is the question of the second form of epistemology. Its solution involves a consideration of such concepts as perception and knowledge, language as expression, truth and falsehood, truth and experience and others, all of which are discussed in Bertrand Russell's book (1965), yet a conference paper does not permit to give them credit in a brief summary.

7. Knowledge, truth and opinion. The only concept which should not be bypassed is 'knowledge' defined by Bertrand

---

[7] "... knowing is a relation of the organism to something else or to a part of itself. Still taking an outside observer's point of view, we may distinguish perceptive awareness from habit-knowledge. Perceptive awareness is a species of 'sensitivity', which is not confined to living organisms, but is also displayed by scientific instruments, and to some degree by everything. Sensitivity consists in behaving, in the presence of a stimulus of a certain kind, in a way in which the animal or thing does not behave in its absence." (p. 11) The difference between these reactions of an instrument and the animate "has to do with 'habit-knowledge'" (p.11). "Every habit involves what, ..., might count as belief in a general law, or even (...) as knowledge of such a law, if the belief happens to be true. /.../ What is called 'learning experience', which is characteristic of living organisms, is the same thing as the acquisition of habits.' (p.11).

Russell as mutual contribution, by the persons involved, toward an accumulation of a sufficiently rich volume of understanding on the point in question. Bertrand Russell relates knowledge to truth and gives priority to the latter: "'truth' is the fundamental concept, and ... 'knowledge' must be defined in terms of 'truth', not vice versa" (p.19). Knowledge "has very vague boundaries" (p.271), but knowledge is obtainable only of "*something* that exists, for what does not exist is nothing" (Russell, 1945, 120). Knowing of absolute beauty is knowledge and knowing of and loving beautiful things means only having opinion. "Thus knowledge is infallible, since it is logically impossible for it to be mistaken. But opinion can be mistaken" (Russell, 1945, 120). It is a consistent requirement therefore to ask a person, who voices an opinion, to explain his evaluation. This is required in reviews, for instance. An explanation provided tests the person's knowledge and indicates his education.

Deliberating the relation between truth and knowledge, the focus centres on language. Every assertion, which may be a sentence or an 'object word' has two sides that must be kept apart: "on the subjective side, the assertion 'expresses' the state of the speaker; on the objective side, it intends to 'indicate' a 'fact' and succeeds in this intention when true. The psychology of belief is concerned only with the subjective side, the question of truth or falsehood also with the objective side" (p.19; cf.: p.p. 163, 168). These concepts and their relations have also been discussed by Bertrand Russell, but I shall sum up briefly only on the question of language in so far as this may give an idea of some prospective turns in the humanities today.

8. Perceiving and recording experience: basic propositions.

As hinted in the above definitions, language permits error in recording scientific observations and in reporting knowledge. What empiricism confirms by observation, epistemology questions. When a scientist records his findings, he must resort to an interpretation of facts available to him, and this interpretation "depends upon very elaborate inductions" (p.15). To believe the scientist, we must draw on "a comparison of his statements with our own experience" (p.15). In its scientific pursuits, epistemology must arrange our beliefs, which we found certain or only probable, in a certain order. First come statements of fact "that are credible independently of any argument in their favour". (Cf. Ogden & Richards, pp. 80-81). These are 'basic propositions' (p.15)

Basic propositions are connected with non-verbal occurrences or 'experiences'. The nature of this connection or the source of the credibility of the basic propositions is one of the fundamental questions of epistemology. Logically, inferential relation matters, yet it is not that of strict deduction. Psychologically, the relation of basic propositions to experiences matters. This relation is the main question in epistemology. It indicates **how responsible any author should be when he generalises on the evidence of his material**.

Formally, the question of **basic propositions** has been resolved by Bertrand Russell. Basic propositions are statements in immediate relation with experience, or "a subclass of epistemological premises... which are caused, as immediately as possible, by perceptive experiences" (Russell, 1965, 130). This author has a special remark on knowledge drawn from a single occurrence and on

"inductions from a number of more or less similar experiences" (p. 130). Bertrand Russell rejects the latter view of empiricists. He holds that man can draw knowledge "from any occurrence that (he) notices", which he can express in sentences if his linguistic habits are adequate. Provided that his linguistic habits are reliable, the truth of his statements "can be wholly dependent upon the character of one occurrence that he is noticing" (p. 130), which produces a basic proposition.

A basic proposition should exclude an opposing opinion, (i.e. to contain no contradictions). It should be clear what a basic proposition can affirm, that is, a statement reporting the subject of immediate perception. The basic proposition should be based on a directly perceivable occurrence and must be independent of inference from other propositions, which gives cause to believe it. A basic proposition must "be of such a form that no other basic proposition can contradict it" (p.131).

9. Propositional attitudes. Apart from 'basic propositions, Bertrand Russell has also analysed sentences of the pattern *I think* *it will rain. I believe that's so.,* which he called **propositional attitudes**. He noted, first, that sentences of this kind seem to resemble propositions but do not behave like ones, and so cause problems to the user of the language and to the analyst[8]. The difficulty with propositional attitudes is that they include two propositions – one of believing and the other, supposedly, of perceiving. "Something believed or doubted or desired can only be expressed by means of a subordinate proposition" (p.155). Even when Bertrand Russell assumes that "we can be aware of believing and desiring something, in just as immediate way as we are aware" of a patch of colour, or that a statement 'I think so' expresses a factual premise as to the person's opinion, the analysis of propositional attitudes offers difficulties (p.155).

Apart from factual premises which become basic propositions and record immediate experience, there are propositions which do not refer to particular events (p.156). These are logical premises, "both deductive and inductive", which are generally admitted (p.156). These logical propositions exclude empirical knowledge, and they are involved in propositional attitudes. In propositional attitudes "we have a complicated mixture of empirical and syntactical questions" (p.159). The opinion side of propositional attitudes can be accounted for by the logic of atomic sentences, which are assertions of the simplest structure, because perception can be excluded from the forms of belief. The proposition in propositional attitudes can be accounted for by the logic of basic propositions.

Thus Bertrand Russell explained the structure, logic and function of the essential sentences in written and spoken language and has strengthened his requirements to the language of science. But science bypasses propositional attitudes and so the logic of basic propositions is sufficient in the language of science.

10. Bertrand Russell summed up his argument in his book by arguing for the reliability of single instances of experience and

---

[8] „In the analysis of what I call ‚propositional attitudes', i.e. occurrences such as believing, doubting, desiring, etc., which are naturally described by sentences containing subordinate sentences, e.g. ‚I think it will rain', we have a complicated mixture of empirical and syntactical questions." (Russell, 1965, 159).

by introducing the principle of mathematical logic: "...on the basis of a single experience, a number of verbal statements are justified", yet only on condition that such statements are "confined to the biography of the speaker", i.e. they should state what a person observes: 'I see a canoid patch of colour', rather than 'there is a dog', because the latter would always involve "some element of inference" or supposition in their justification (Russell, 1965, 19). His consecutive conclusion in logical analysis, for epistemology of the first type, was that "So long as your words merely describe present experiences, the sole possible errors are linguistic, and these only involve socially wrong behaviour, not falsehood" (Russell, 1965, 77). What has been said of Bertrand Russell's reasoning of and requirements to language in use indicates once again that the language of scholarly papers has to be very disciplined and logical, and this is what most papers published in the humanities in Lithuania lack. **The raising of requirements to the language of scholarly papers would definitely improve publications in the humanities.** People in the humanities in Lithuania have again to accept the criticism of today silently as they have lived long enough taking no heed of what has been known of language and philosophy for seventy years and what could have disciplined and improved their publications steering them away from the present publication explosion of the quality beyond criticism.

11. The relevance of the historical conceptions to the present-day humanities. Yet not to lose the attention of the audience, I have to say how this philosophy relates to the humanities. The question of how we know that the basic propositions and the supporting experience are credible applies most delicately to research in the humanities, primarily to language study and research. It is a fixed requirement that any paper in language and literature study should be based on appropriate material, yet what is being published shows that such material is very elementary and little analysed or not analysed at all, just summed up statistically. Analysis of meaning in any study must be the founding step as an aspect of interpretation, especially if we remember Ogden and Richards' claim of the uselessness of "the futile study of forms" (Ogden & Richards, p.45) and if we take into consideration at least the founding concepts of the functional theory of language. Without any further criticism, I can assuredly claim that the analysis, in any paper in the humanities, should rest on the previous detailed analysis of the material, which, to be credible, **requires very proficient knowledge of the language**. I would leave this as a rhetorical question but I should strongly insist that numbers of publications in the humanities locally and globally, bypass this requirement to the language knowledge of the author. What has so far helped us to escape and survive is the fact that few readers were deeply concerned with what they had read to voice any criticism and that we have safely lived on because humanities are not a life science and the authors' errors in them do not threaten death to anyone. However, it has started to threaten our finances. If this is a bomb thrown into the humanities' garden, we must accept it and see to its soft landing for the reasons just stated.

12. Semiotic criteria for the analysis of verbal communication in the humanities. Whatever the fallacies and whatever the fundamental credibility of philosophical explanations of the fallibility of language as the requirements to the language of science, the three types of codes enumerated above are supposed to "correspond broadly to three key kinds of knowledge required to interpreters of a text, namely, knowledge of: 1) the world (social knowledge), 2) the medium or the genre (textual knowledge), 3) the relationship between (1) and (2) (modality judgments)" (Chandler, 2007, 150). I shall take these kinds of knowledge into consideration in my interpretation of communication in the humanities analysed basically by the method of binary oppositions.

My ultimate goal is to reappraise[9] the humanities as an educational programme. I shall draw conclusions arguing from

---

[9] We are familiar with the positive appraisal of the humanities by classical scholars who, in the University of Vilnius, are active to extend the programmes of the classical languages and classical culture in schools motivated by an honest and unshakable belief that classical studies can "elevate the culture of our society, fortify the foundations of general education, contribute to the fostering of a mature, harmonious and active citizen as an individual" (Ulčinaitė, 2011, 2; cf.: Adomėnas, 2011). Experienced and very well educated scholars in modern languages and literature are of the same opinion of the humanities. Students still flock to get MA degrees and diplomas in the humanities, but governments,

the founding principles of semiotics. Referring to Roman Jakobson's concept of the integrity of linguistics given even the most radical changes in it, Jurij Lotman started his reasoning of the semiotics of culture from the fundamental notion that "a combination of homeostatics[10] and dynamism (is) a proof of the integrity and vitality of a theory which is capable to revise essentially both its interior organization and the system of its relations with other "disciplines" (Lotman, 2004, 59). My question today is **whether the humanities have retained their integrity** in the chaos, changes and reforms of the present-day.

I shall base my conclusions on an analytical summary of the value of published works in the humanities and of instruction in university while choosing single items as illustrative examples. In addition to applying codes[11] drawn from semiotics (see p. 4, above) for the initial evaluation of the material, even when their operation is not easy to notice and recognise (Chandler, 2007, 173), I have identified items of my material according to two more general categories – broadcast and narrow cast codes[12]. Although I share Daniel Chandler's notion that "everything in human culture and communication … cannot simply be reduced to the operation of semiotic codes" (Chandler, 2007, 173), applying the codes like parametres initially orientates a researcher in what he can expect from and what he can find in his further textual analysis.

I shall briefly review and sum up my findings on the following material: one monograph by a British philosopher, Mary Midgley, two books and a teaching aid written by three Lithuanian authors, unnamed articles written by teachers in Lithuania, instructions written to teachers in Lithuania, verbal

---

organisations and lay persons, who are not idle, condemn the humanities as degraded and not worth the money. I mean to reappraise the humanities minding this rift in opinion.

[10] Homeostatics is stability and equilibrium in an organic system (cf.: W'sNWD, p. 671). Here, homeostatics is equivalent to synchrony, whereas dynamism to diachrony.

[11] "Codes are not simply 'conventions' of communication but rather procedural *systems* of related conventions which operate in certain domains" (Chandler, 2007, 148).

[12] It is John Fiske who "distinguishes between *broadcast* codes, which are shared by members of a mass audience, and *narrowcast* codes which are aimed at a more limited audience; pop music is a broadcast code; ballet is a narrowcast code" (Chandler, 2007, 170-171; Fiske, 1998, 91-95).

instruction in the classroom on the interpretation of text and snatches of routine communication in the context of humanities. My question would be the following: **what does textual material** current in the sphere of humanities **witness of their integrity and quality**.

Methodologically, I have been guided by the following binary oppositions in assessing the content and value of the items in my analysis, which have been drawn from the dynamic model of a semiotic system, were employed and exploited in the semiotic study of culture:

1) synchronic and diachronic aspects;
2) systemic *vs* non-systemic constituents;
3) monomeaningful *vs* ambivalent constituents;
4) the opposition nucleus *vs* periphery;
5) the opposition described *vs* undescribed;
6) the opposition obligatory *vs* optional;
7) the opposition of primary *vs* secondary information (Lotman, 2004, 60-75).

In her book, *The Myths We Live By,* Mary Midgley (2007) deliberates how ideas change in history and become myths under the effect of ideologies, which itself she considers to be a myth, or by crumbling in time under the influence of exaggerated expectations. She analyses how three myths – the social contract myth, the progress myth and the myth of omnicompetent science – began and degraded down to the state of frustrated expectances. The <u>diachronic measurement</u> shapes Mary Midgley's study structurally with interpolations of synchronic descriptions and of facts at definite points in time. This study is <u>systemic</u> historically, philosophically and argumentatively. Its terms and key concepts are <u>monomeaningful</u> and the argument leads to grounded and convincing conclusions, yet does not exclude digressions to individual <u>ambivalent</u> interpretations related to the present day.

As a study in philosophy, *The Myths We Live By* cannot be firmly placed in the centre in philosophy or in the periphery, which would be the popularisation of philosophy. It is an expert humanitarian study accessible and relevant to all students in the humanities. It is a study of wide currency, yet not designed in the broadcast code. Its design ensures its quality.

In terms of the opposition described *vs* undescribed, the assessment of *The Myths We Live By* would depend on the addressee: it would be educating and enlightening to students in the humanities. It would not be wholly so to professors holding degrees in philosophy. However, like her other book (Midgley, 2006), it is necessary to students in the humanities today whose sense of history is in atrophy and that of philosophy is vague.

In terms of the opposition obligatory *vs* optional, the structure of this study by Mary Midgley integrates deeply the facts selected as its constituents. The redundancy of this study is minimal yet present in the personal rather than strictly logical aspect of the narrative. While not to be used as a textbook, *The Myths We Live By* would be relevant to students inclined to individual study and to those rejecting classroom instruction. While not exactly obligatory in the humanities, this study is likely to involve the young in meaningful discussions of scholarly ideas. (An aside on superficial knowledge of history)

This book combines both primary and secondary information, which is most welcome in education. Its primary information is subject to dynamism in the author's reasoning and the presentation of secondary information involves and enlightens the reader as the author reaches out to the less informed while sharing her knowledge of history and philosophy in the register accessible to university students. The applied aspect of *The Myths We Live By* qualifies this study as a contribution to the perception and treatment of conceptual heritage of Western society, to education and to the culture of modern society.

13. Publications in the humanities in Lithuania will be reviewed anonymously. Three papers (A, B, & C) will hold my attention, all three representing the textual code and being written in the narrowcast code. One study (Paper A) in language and style analyses how style in language may be defined with reference to the linguistic theory of the second half of the twentieth century and looks into the necessity to particularise the theory when it is applied to the description of the constituents of style. The linguistic theory is summed up comprehensively, uses of language as the "little described" functional aspect of the theory are elaborated on and the basic concepts of style defined.

It is a <u>synchronic study</u> of the subject while the diachronic aspect features only in evaluations of stylistic features described in the studies of the twentieth century. The argument is consecutive and systemic theoretically as there is no division of form and meaning in the theory. The terms are monomeaningful and unambiguously defined: the conclusions are grounded and there is no ambivalence in the treatment of the phenomenon of style. The language of this study, though, yet requires general editing, which is its major drawback.

Because of the small volume, the focus is on key and therefore nucleus concepts of style, which are defined unambiguously and with the required theoretical consistency. The periphery of the subject is largely ignored because of its limited volume. The opposition <u>described *vs* undescribed</u> applies to Paper A in the sense that the traditionally described concepts of style are either used or appear irrelevant while the new concepts are described and originally defined. The opposition <u>obligatory *vs* optional</u> is neutralised by the novelty of the approach and what is described is relevant to the subject. Its content qualifies it as necessary in language and style studies. The paper wholly is necessary and can be applied in education yet would be more useful as a book for teachers rather than as a textbook for students because of its narrowcast code.

Paper A includes the transmission of both <u>primary and secondary information</u>. As it draws on an original linguistic theory, it transmits secondary information, which is required in education. As the paper elaborates on an aspect of the theory and defines the key concepts of style as meaning, it transmits primary information. This opposition is balanced, as requires a paper of an applied character. It contributes to quality education and sets an example of a comprehensive monograph in applied linguistics which may be used in teaching. (An aside on textbooks)

Another paper in literary studies (Paper B) and one more in linguistics (Paper C) are interesting because they open up with statements that the subject and the phenomenon have not been and cannot yet be defined. This fixes the stance of distrust in the reader from the beginning. In both there is an attempt to follow <u>the synchronic approach,</u> but while it is impossible to ignore the diachronic aspect in study related to literature (Paper B), the historical aspect features visibly in it, while, in the linguistic paper (Paper C), the diachronic aspect is ignored because of the limited volume and point of view. The first author (Paper B) purports to credit history but does it so impressionistically that almost fails in her attempt. The second author (Paper C) sets a task for herself to compare the phenomenon in focus in two languages and does it to an extent.

With respect to the opposition systemic *vs* non-systemic, Paper B cannot be evaluated: its subject matter is not defined and its historical aspect is fragmented. The author of Paper C does explain aspects of the linguistic phenomenon in focus, so that the invariant and indispensable constituents are described. Variant constituents are only mentioned, which is their right treatment.

With respect to the opposition monomeaningful *vs* ambivalent, Paper B is blank because its subject is not described and no concepts listed or defined. Its ambivalence is obvious because the value of its recurrent constituents/concepts has to be deduced by the reader and the result would definitely depend on his erudition and on the selections he makes. It is also the reader who can define what is monomeaningful and what is ambivalent in Paper B. As the subject of the linguistic Paper C is virtually defined, its description has a set of monomeaningful concepts that cover the nucleus of the object of description and its ambivalence is respectively inconsiderable.

With respect to the opposition described *vs* undescribed, both Papers B & C focus on the subjects researched to an extent yet lacking comprehensive works which are required in education. None, however, has this aim accomplished because the author of the literary Paper B does not define nor outline its object, while the linguistic Paper C describes its object satisfactorily within a very narrow range.

With respect to the opposition obligatory *vs* optional (redundant), Paper B does not qualify at all as it can be used only by a further researcher because of its unargumented, unreviewed and fragmented references presented like excursions to bibliographical items. It is up to every reader to decide what is necessary and what is redundant in it. On my part, I should point out metaphoric expression throughout, emotive quotations and impressionistic reasoning, all of which are redundant to me educated in the written tradition of the Anglo-Saxons. Paper C, which holds its nucleus concepts together, indicates that there is key constituents in it which are necessary and its small volume saves it from much redundancy.

In so far as <u>primary *vs* secondary information</u> is concerned, Paper B rests entirely on secondary information, little analysed, too, and linguistic Paper C rests basically on the primary data of two languages, which is not exactly primary information. Both papers are vulnerable on the point of this opposition.

The narrowcast code of Papers B & C limit their use to specialists/students in the humanities: the emotive and impressionistic presentation does not buy Paper B a place in the subject its title claims, while a narrow range of the object and limited research does earn Paper C the status of a textbook. Therefore Paper B can be best used only as a bibliographical guide and Paper C as a teaching aid.

Unnamed articles written by teachers in Lithuania merit a very brief assessment. The papers I have read identified no real problem in language studies, they did not outline the context of their research nor did they report on sufficient data or experience in the way required in an acceptable paper in scholarship. I wrote positive reviews guided by an unwritten rule that a reviewer is obliged to promote the author and if he cannot, he should not take up reviewing. As I could not refuse reviewing, I wrote positive reviews. But I have remembered this case of corruption and should say today that no papers produced piecemeal should be published in the humanities. This applies to papers written by teachers in Lithuania. The publishing criterion in the qualification of teachers should be profitably abandoned.

14. Instructions written to teachers in Lithuania fare no better. I have been familiar with two documents:
(Užsienio kalbų bendroji programa pagrindinei mokyklai. Metodinės rekomendacijos. Written by six women teachers. The version of March 2009. Dalyko ir užsienio kalbos integruoto mokymosi gairės. Projektas. CLIL LR Šmm. The version of November 2013). The first document was a copy of CEFR, although CEFR stipulates that its articles should be adapted for concrete schools and their

particular aims: „2. One thing should be made clear right away. We have NOT set out to tell practitioners what to do, or how to do it. We are raising questions, not answering them. It is not the funciton of the Common European Framework to lay down the objectives that users should pursue or the methods they should employ." (CEFR, p.2). „5.2.1 /.../ This is the approach adopted in Section 4.2. It attempts to identify and classify the main components of linguistic competences as knowledge of, and ability to use, the formal resources from which well-formed, meaningful messages may be assembled and formulated. The scheme that follows aims only to offer as classificatory tools some parameters and categories which may be found useful for the description of the linguistic content and as a basis for reflection. Those practitioners who prefer to use a different frame of reference are free, here as everywhere, to do so." (CEFR, p.109).

As I was reading this document and got to the article of competences, I could not take in its content as

„Methodological recommendations for the basic school". Cf.: „2.2. Komunikacinė kalbinė kompetencija Lingvistinę kompetenciją sudaro: leksinė kompetencija – žinios ir gebėjimai vartoti žodyną; gramatinė kompetencija – gramatinių išteklių išmanymas ir sugebėjimas jais naudotis;semantinė kompetencija – mokinio gebėjimas suvokti ir kurti reikšmes; fonologinė kompetencija – mokinio žinios ir gebėjimai suprasti ir produkuoti kalbos garsų vienetus, žodžio sudėtį, kirtį, intonaciją; ortografinė kompetencija – mokinio gebėjimas suvokti ir produkuoti rašytinius tekstus; ortoepinė kompetencija – mokinio gebėjimas tinkamai ištarti žodžius pagal jų rašytinę formą."

I was shaken as no university could ever accomplish these competences as defined for decades and for at least one class of students. I could do no less than jot down my own version of this parlance.

Cf.: leksinė kompetencija – mokėti ir aktyviai vartoti bendrinės kalbos žodyno minimumą; įsiminti ir suprasti plačios apimties pasyvų žodyną; gramatinė kompetencija – įsiminti pagrindinių gramatinių struktūrų reikšmes ir mokėti tas struktū-ras vartoti; išmanyti sintaksės modelių variantus ir mokėti pasirinkti jų minimumą; semantinė kompetencija – suprasti ir įsiminti, kad ir žodžiai, ir gramatinė struktūros vienodai reikšmingi; fonetinė kompetencija – sugebėjimas taisyklingai tarti garsus junginiuose (žodžiuose) ir prasmin-gai intonuoti; ortografinė kompetencija – išmokti taisyklingos rašybos; ortoepinė kompetencija – išsilavinti taisyklingą literatūrinę tartį.

(An aside on the qualifications of the writers and on instructions based on hearsay. A comment on the second document, which is favourable as the authors sought improvement).

There have been also hearsay instructions in universities in Lithuania. „Some of them went as follows: „They say that now the students' psychological comfort should be uppermost in the teacher's mind, that the teacher should regulate even his tone of voice not to discourage the students and not to use red ink to mark the students' papers, which may be damaging psychologically...", etc.

It was only in Thomas Langtry's paper that I have learned of the constructivist and congintivist theories with respective referentes and found out that some thinking had gone on before the focus has to shift from knowledge to confort in the classroom. Instructions based on hearsay are vicious because they degrade the teacher while putting prescriptions before knowledge and reasoning.

15. Verbal instruction in the classroom in the interpretation of text is an easily damaged activity in the present–day humanities for two reasons – the inspiration that literary texts give to the interpreter and a likely superficiality that ensues. Superficial and light-minded comments in interpretations given by teachers of little education are likely to convey to the inexperienced listeners, (and secondary school pupils are listeners of this group), that interpretation of text means saying whatever one chooses and parading it with enjoyment. (A comment recounting Plato's concept).

I really wonder how many young and inexperienced **teachers of today**, who are so much valued by adminstrations at present, **have demonstrated such ignorance** publicly and **have moved their students to so false an impression.** If only one group of students have had so false an expereince, much damage has been done to their education and to the humanities in the Republic. If this happens to happen, the teachers' education has to be improved, especially their knowledge of the language, and the use of interpretation to young students has to be seriously reconsidered. **My further question is whether teachers themselves have contributed to the degrading of the humanities in the Republic, and I would tend to give a positive answer to this question.**

A lecturer's challenge in the classroom has been very sensitively described by Roland Bartes when he said that a lecturer at the rostrum „relives the painful strain of his research as he voices his results rather than delivers instruction from a ready body of internalised knowledge" (Bartes, 1989,546). A lecturer has to be very well informed yet very disciplined to limit his use of terms and statements so as to facilitate the process of learning.

16. Snatches of routine communication in the context of humanities include the following folk wisdom in my material:

1. „We want quality education."= „Mes norim kokybiškų žinių." (A young student advertised on the Lithuanian TV in 2012-13, who campaigned for reforms in higher education on behalf of the body of the students of the Republic).

2. „Don't you prescribe that elitist education to our children. The children are exhausted as they are." = Nekiškit to elitinio išsilavinimo mūsų vaikams. Vaikai ir taip persitempę." (A male commentator on www.delfi.lt, in response to the article by Mantas Adomėnas (2011), in 2011.

3. The school coaches a flock of parrots: it teaches to reproduce borrowed thoughts rather than critical thinking." = „Mokykla ugdo papūgų bandą: moko ne kritinio mąstymo, o atkartoti svetimas mintis." (A comment to a photo at:

www.15min.lt/naujiena/aktualu/lietuva /dalios-grybauskaites-achilo-kulnas-... - 10 April 2014).

4. „They will not, in all likelihood, read „War and Peace",
   but their technical skills are really developed, for instance,
   it's nothing for a first grader to present his holiday
   impressions in Power Point slides." = „„Karo ir taikos"
   jie, ko gero, neskaitys, bet jų techniniai įgūdžiai tikrai
   išlavinti, pavyzdžiui, pirmokui visai nesudėtinga savo
   atostogų įspūdžius pristatyti Power Point skaidrėse." At:
   www.15min.lt/naujiena/aktualu/lietuva/prasta-klasikine-pedagogika-siandienei-z-kartai-nebetinka-56-423630 - 21
   March 2014.

5. (A university teacher to a prospective postgraduate in the
   humanities): „Perrašinėsi knygas." (= "You'll be a scribe
   all right .") (Vilnius, 1969).

6. (University secretaries of a man taking up research in the
   humanities): „Kažin ką jis neparašys, ar vertėjo?" – „Bus
   užsiėmęs, ir gerai." (= „He will not produce anything
   much. Was it worth it?" – „He will be engaged, that's
   fine.") (Vilnius, c. 1975).

7. „...Oginskį iš esmės galima laikyti kolaborantu." (Jūratė
   Mičiulienė. Politinis M.K.Oginskio polonezas Europoje.
   „Lietuovs žinios", Nr.80, 2014 04 25, p.11).

These quotations reflect the milieu in which professionals in the
humanities function in the Republic. All of them are instances of
emotive or misdirected language, that is the language which
Ogden and Richards termed as the emotive use of words and of
which they warned to beware. As this is not true in the strict
scientific sense, according to the judgment of the same authors, it
cannot be intelligibly discussed. So comments like these should
be dismissed rather than argued about. Nevertheless they pollute
the atmopshere in the humanities. Some of these quotations (1)
illustrate cliché in communication, which appears in broadcast
(restricted) codes (Chandler, 2007, 170). When so far-fetched
utterances as the quotation under (1) are used as a challenge, the
attacked are confused. Cliché can be impressive down to a loss of
immediate reflection and, consequently, to the absence of a
response. This was in actual fact the initial effect of the public

blackmail which quotation (1) elicited. It is not easy to counter a cliché because this requires a documented argument. Professors and academicians of the Republic did produce an argument, yet it cost a period of tortured silence on the part of the attacked educationists, as Lithuanian TV viewers can remember. It may have been no less authority than Bertrand Russell who prompted a response with his definition of knowledge quoted above.

The last quotation (7) illustrates the quality of the qualification of authors publishing in the media. The authors of today very often treat historical personalities and their views having placed them squarely on the desk of today and admit this kind of absurd statements. Opinions like this, moreover, given without supplying reasons for the judgment, which is obligatory to a person of good education, circulate and shape the views of society, which, then, influence culture in schools and scholarship.

17. Conclusions.

Giving answers to the questions which I asked in this paper, the fact that humanities have lost the people aspiring to perfect education is the first testimony of why the foundations in the humanities have become questionable.The foundations potentially exist yet there is nuobody or very few to pursue the former ideals associated with the humanities. The concept of the potential of humanitaran education has changed and, with it, their foundations and integrity.

My analysis has prompted the following requirements to follow:

1) Publications in the humanities should be written by professionals holding degrees, and following the requirements to their langauge set by Bertrand Russell and Algirdas Greimas.

2) Publications as a criterion in teachers' education should be abandoned. There can be other ways and means to improve the teachers' qualification. Teachers' education does call for improvement, with language and literature to become priorities.

3) Language knowledge of the teachers should be advanced or of near-native proficiency.

4) Classroom teaching should improve with the improvement of the teachers' education.

5) The influence and administration of laymen in the humanities should be rejected. Professionals in modern languages and literatures in the Republic have the model of the campaigning Lithuanian classicists to follow in academic work and that of physicists and mathematicians[13] in research and decision making.

These concluding statements in no way mean a prison-house for the humanities. Wit in Bertrand Russell's book at points (1965, 13, 156, 322) shows that a very responsible scientist can permit himself good humour without degrading his work and without following the MA level prescriptions given to professors in the humanities in Lithuania.

Like Thomas Langtry, I would encourage no more reforms, only perfection, balance and harmony in improvements. Even if we may not be aware of our possessions, other people in high places tell us that we have talent and resources to see to resurrection in the humanities. It might be helpful to give a shake to the methods of teaching through the teachers' cooperation rather than institutional reforms. A Republican Project for the teachers willing to publish might be worked out following the requirements highlighted in this paper for the willing to find a place and to do the work in. The problem „is not in our stars, / But in ourselves, that we are underlings".

---

[13] My reference here is to a report, 'Exacaster. Big data: 3 years of fun', given by Šarūnas Chomentauskas (www.exacaster.com) at the Conference 'Big Data Strategy' on the 29th of May 2014 in Vilnius, Lithuania. This speaker elaborated on the work with and results on big data in designing projects and working out their execution. He noted three stages in the work from generalizations on data analysis, to predicting results and setting to action while being true to the findings rather than to the complaining. This triad sums up as understanding, predicting, taking action, well applicable in the humanities, the people in which often lose clear vision of the important stages, discipline in decision making and determination in action. This is not saying too much. If we mind that "the chief use of humanistic studies is to explain, to understand, to appreciate" (Goodman, 1971, 137), parallels between the mathematician's reasoning and the requirements in humanitarian scholarship will not be far to seek. Language will again be the object and means and the execution will depend on dedication and determination.

Referentes

Adomėnas, Mantas, 2001 – Lietuvos mokykla: keistis negalima taisktytis   //
http://www.lt/news/rings/politics/madomėnas... - 1 June 2011

Bartes, Roland, 1989 – Selected Papers; Semiotics, Poetics.(In Russian) – Moscow: „Progress". – 615p.

Chandler, Daniel, 2007 – Semiotics. The Basics. – London and New York: Routledge. – xviii, 307p.

Drazdauskiene, Marija Liudvika, 2011 – Language and Thought: Influence, Challenge and Interaction. MS.

Fiske, John, 1998 – Įvadas į komunikacijos studijas (in Lithuanian). – Vilnius: „Baltos lankos". – 239p.

Goodman, Paul, 1971 – Speaking and Language: The Defence of Poetry. – New York: Random House. – 242p.

Greimas, Algirdas J., 1971 – Bendrosios semiotikos problemos. In: Iš arti ir iš toli. – Vilnius: „Vaga", 1991, 38-59.

Greimas, Algirdas J., 1977 – O visgi kalba ką nors reiškia. In: Iš arti ir iš toli. – Vilnius: „Vaga", 1991, 72-80.

Greimas, Algirdas J., 1985 – Intelektualinės biografijos bandymas. In: Iš arti ir iš toli. – Vilnius: „Vaga", 1991, 18-37.

Halliday, M.A.K., 1973 – Explorations in the Functions of Language. – London: Arnold. – 140p.

Halliday, M.A.K., 1976 – Sistem and Function in Language/ Edited by Gunther Kress. – Oxford: Oxford University Press. – 374p.

Langtry, Thomas, B.A., M.A., 2014 – Relevance of Liberal Arts in Twenty-First Century Academics: Notes for „Questionable Foundations and Quality in the Humanities", a Lecture by Dr Marija Liudvika Drazdauskiene, Professor at Wszechnica Polska, for Presentation June 2014 in Lithuania – MS, 2014 RelevanceOfLiberalArts2.26.2014.Langtry.pdf

Lotman, Jurij, 2004 – Kultūros semiotika. – Vilnius: „Baltos lankos". – 366p.

Matthews, Peter H., 1997 – The Oxford Concise Dictionary of Linguistics – Oxford and New York: OUP.- x, 410p.

Midgley, Mary, 2006 – Science and Poetry. – London and New York: Routledge. – xiv, 314p.

Midgley, Mary, 2007 – The Myths We Live By. – London and New York: Routledge. – x, 192p.

Plato, 1938 – Ion. In: The Classical Thinkers on Art (in Russian). – Moskva: Iskusstvo. – 65-77.

Russell, Bertrand, 1965 (1949) – An Inquiry into Meaning and Truth. – Harmondsworth: Penguin. – 333p.

Russell, Bertrand, 1945 – A History of Western Philosophy. – New York: Simon and Schuster. – 842p.

The 7 Liberal Arts – trivium, quadrivium and logical fallacies (n.d.). Retrieved from: http://www.matrixwissen.de/index.php?option=com_content&view=article&id=275:the-7-liberal-arts-trivium-quadrivium-and-logical-fallcies&catid=145:die-7-freien-kuenste&Itemid=124&Lang=en – 24 April 2014 m. gegužė 30 d.

Ulčinaitė, Eugenija, 2011 (20110) – Klasikinių kalbų reikšmė ir vaidmuo ugdant asmenybę // Literatūra ir menas, Nr. 4 (3316), 2011 01 28. p.2.

Widdowson, Henry G., 1992 – Practical Stylistics. An Approach to {Poetry. – Oxford: OUP. – Xiv, 230p.

,Wrong Way Corrigan', 2013 www.corrigan.blogspot.com/2013/01/a-qualified-uneducated-elite.html – 27 April 2014